COLOR CREATIONS IN BUTTERCREAM

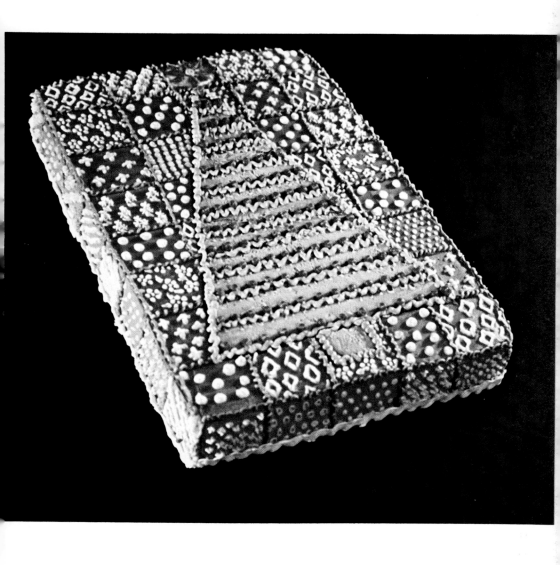

Color
Creations IN
BUTTERCREAM

Richard V. Snyder

Owner and Director
The Snyder Studio of Cake Decoration
Detroit, Michigan

ILLUSTRATED IN COLOR

An Exposition-Banner Book

Exposition Press   Hicksville, New York

To
CARLENE M. SNYDER,
my wife and dearest friend,
with love and appreciation

FIRST EDITION

Library of Congress Catalog Card Number: 75-46425

ISBN 0-682-48458-X

Printed in the United States of America

CONTENTS

PREFACE

Decorating Cakes for Fun and Profit was published in 1953. In 1955 *27 Special Creations for Cake Decorators* was published as a workbook to be used with the textbook.

65 Buttercream Flowers, a very different kind of textbook, appeared in 1957. It was intended to expand the repertoire of flowers used in cake decoration. This was followed by *29 New Floral Creations* in 1962 and *28 More Floral Creations* in 1963. These paperbacks were published as idea books to supplement the work in *65 Buttercream Flowers*.

In 1958 Mr. and Mrs. Dalquist, owners of The Maid of Scandinavia Company in Minneapolis and publishers of *Mail Box News*, a hobby magazine for cake decorators, started a Snyder series of illustrated articles which appeared about eleven times a year. Many articles at first were revised reprints of material that had appeared in my books. Gradually new material was created.

However, students and magazine readers have found it difficult, if not impossible, to locate the new techniques and creations which have evolved during the past seventeen years. *Color Creations in Buttercream* contains all the new techniques and most of the creations which have appeared in *Mail Box News* but have not been published in any of my other books.

The first five chapters deal with new techniques and should be studied first. The rest of the book is devoted to new creations based upon these techniques and those taught in my previous books.

In order to make the text as useful as possible, there is an "Index for Chapters I-V," an "Index of Creations by Title for Chapters VI-XIX," and an "Index of Creations by Flowers and Greenery for Chapters VI-XIX." As a further effort toward coordination, there is a "General Index of 27, 28, and 29 Creations by Title" and a "General Index of 27, 28, and 29 Creations by Flowers and Greenery."

The 55 new creations in this book include 58 kinds of flowers and greenery. The 84 creations previously published in *27, 28, and 29 Creations* include 66 kinds of flowers and greenery, some of them different from those in our new book, so that in all 139 creations there are 86 varieties of flowers and greenery. The appendixes will be a rich source of suggestions and ideas for amateurs and professionals alike.

9

Frequent references are made to the different books, according to the following code:

DC Decorating Cakes for Fun and Profit
BCF 65 Buttercream Flowers
27C 27 Special Creations for Cake Decorators
28C 28 More Floral Creations for Cake Decorators
29C 29 New Floral Creations for Cake Decorators
CC Color Creations in Buttercream

(Note that in page references, f. following a page number means "and the following page," and ff. "and the following pages.")

Illustrations are numbered consecutively throughout the book. In the first five chapters black and white pictures are used with the text. Nineteen of the illustrations in the remaining chapters are black and white, but they are repeated in color, the same numbers being used with the addition of the letter C. The pictures are cross-referenced within the text.

Grateful acknowledgment is made to Mr. and Mrs. Mark Dalquist, publishers of *Mail Box News*, to Mrs. Char Brown, editor of *Mail Box News*, to Mr. William C. Tucker of the Grossman-Knowling Company, Detroit, who made many of the excellent photographs, and to Carlene M. Snyder, who, as a patient book widow, once again contributed ideas, objective criticism, and encouragement.

RICHARD V. SNYDER

COLOR CREATIONS
IN BUTTERCREAM

FIG. 1

I

LILIES

SMALL BUTTERCREAM EASTER LILIES

Throughout this book and our previous books use only the recipes given on pp. 191-192 for buttercream decorating icing. Use only a high-ratio, all-vegetable oil shortening for best results.

These small buttercream Easter lilies can be made, frozen, and used on a cake within a few minutes. This is an advantage over royal icing lilies of any size, or the usual large buttercream lilies, which require a minimum of 24-hours' drying time before they can be used. If desired, this small buttercream variety can also be made up in advance and stored for future use.

Take 2-inch squares of waxed paper, fold them into quarters, and cut them into circles. Make one cut from edge to center of each circle. (Fig. 1.)

Make a cone of waxed paper and fasten it with icing so that three-fourths of it is double thickness.

After adding a little icing to inside of small plastic bell mold, press paper cone firmly against inner surface of bell.

Using a ¼-inch V-cone of white buttercream icing, and *tilting the bell on its side*, make a leaflike, tapered petal from the bottom to the top of the waxed-paper cone.

(*Note:* In Fig. 1 the cones were removed from the bell for the sake of photographic clarity. In actual practice leave the cone in the bell mold until all six petals are made.)

Space two more tapered petals so that the result will resemble a three-bladed propeller. (Turn the bell mold each time so that the petal is made against the lower side of the mold.)

Make three more petals between the original three. (Keep the bell mold tilted on its side as you work.)

Take cone out of bell and place base of cone in a small ball of icing. Make pistil in flower center with a No. 2 yellow-green cone. Make six stamens with a No. 2 yellow cone. Brush tops of stamens with red or brown liquid vegetable color. (An alternate method is to add pistil and stamens after the lily is frozen and in the arrangement. This makes it possible to stabilize the inside of an imperfect flower with some white icing before adding the center.)

Place lilies in the freezer for five minutes.

In the meantime pipe a stem with a No. 3 medium green cone. Make leaves with a ¼-inch V-cone of light green icing.

Remove frozen lilies from papers and place them in arrangement.

Use a No. 5 cone of very soft white icing to lengthen lilies. Using a brush and water, join icings together smoothly. Brush very light green liquid vegetable color at the base of each lily.

Bring No. 2 medium green stems to each lily from top of main stem. Make buds with No. 3 medium green and No. 5 white cones.

As petals thaw, curve the points outward and downward slightly with your fingers.

LARGE BUTTERCREAM EASTER LILIES (Fast Method)

This new method for making large buttercream Easter lilies is much easier and faster than the one described in my *65 Buttercream Flowers*.

Use paper towel for cones in lily nail because it will be absorbent and will speed the drying process. (Fig. 2.)

Make 4-inch squares. Fold them in half. Fold them in half again. Round the loose edges with scissors. Open them up. Cut from edge to center.

Use white buttercream icing in a No. 70 leaf cone and a No. 12 lily nail.

Put icing on one side of cut edge of paper circle.

Move iced edge underneath rest of paper circle until three-fourths of cone is double thickness. Press together so that cone will keep its shape.

Put some icing in nail to make paper cone stick to it.

Press cone firmly into the top of the No. 12 nail.

Holding the nail so that one side will be horizontal where each petal is being made, make lily as illustrated here, and as taught in *65 Buttercream Flowers*, pp. 88ff. (Fig. 3.)

FIG. 2

Make holes in bottoms of small paper cups, or use some other form of drying rack.

Place each lily in a second, smaller (3-inch square) paper towel cone to speed the drying process, and then place it in a drying rack of some sort.

Using scissors, cut between petals so that outside cone papers will allow tops of petals to curve outward in a graceful fashion.

Taper the points of the petals by hand wherever they need it. If a particular petal is hopeless, make a new petal on top of the old one. (No one will know.)

Make a No. 2 stiff, light yellow-green pistil in the center of each lily and six yellow or amber No. 2 stamens around each pistil.

The lilies will dry in a period of twelve hours or less. If unusual weather conditions prevail, freeze flowers for four or five minutes before removing them from paper cones. They will not collapse if they have been dried first.

FIG. 3

Use a No. 5 cone of *very soft* white icing to lengthen lilies when they are placed in arrangement. Using a brush and water, join icings together smoothly. Brush very light green liquid vegetable color at the base of each lily.

See *BCF*, pp. 90f., for method of natural arrangement with stems and leaves.

II
TREES

BUTTERCREAM TREE

The light brown trunk and branches are made with soft buttercream icing in a No. 4 cone and with figure-piping technique. (Fig. 4.) Move the edge of the tube back and forth against the surface of the brown icing to make it look like rough bark.

To represent leaves appropriate for fall, variegate a No. 27 star cone

FIG. 4

with several colors of buttercream icing: medium green, light green, yellow, orange, and a touch of red and brown.

Minimize the star effect as much as possible by holding tube close to the icing when exerting pressure. Notice that branches tend to taper toward the ends. Leave open spaces now and then between branches. Let parts of the brown tree trunk and branches show occasionally.

In the winter put only a few brown leaves on the bare branches. Add a little soft white icing to the tops of the branches to represent snow. Using clear piping gel, hang some icicles from the branches.

In the spring and summer variegate different shades of green in the star cone and put a bird's nest among the leaves. Then figure pipe a few birds and a squirrel or two.

How about a tree house?

You will find many uses for buttercream trees.

EVERGREEN TREES

Evergreen trees can be used as decorations on the tops or sides of cakes. They can be made directly on the cake, or they can be made in advance and frozen or dried before they are placed on a cake. The ones pictured in Fig. 5 are made with buttercream. Royal icing can be used in much the same way.

Make the trunk 3 inches high with a No. 5 cone of soft gray-brown icing.

Using a 3/16-inch V-cone of green icing, hold cone so that cone opening is vertical (on edge) and at right angles to the trunk. Bring leaflike branches away from trunk and up slightly. Keep edge of cone against surface.

Form branches that are between the surface and a vertical position (diagonal branches). Then form branches that come toward you and up slightly.

For variation that resembles Scotch pine, add No. 13 green stars to edges of branches.

Add little dots of brown to indicate pine cones, and add some white icing to tops of branches to suggest snow.

Make little icicles on branches with clear piping gel.

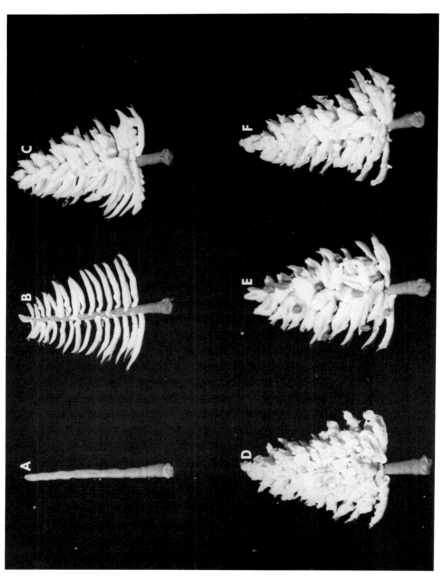

FIG. 5

III

WREATHS
AND CORSAGES

TWELVE-POINT WREATH

Before starting work on this chapter, it would be helpful to review the section on wreath arrangement in *DC*, pp. 62ff.

The models used in Fig. 6 are small circles of white cardboard, 3½ inches in diameter. The dots are formed with a No. 2 cone of green icing; the stems with a No. 1 cone. Any size round cake or cake dummy can be used for practice. If an 8-inch or larger cake is used, a No. 2 or 3 tube will probably be used for the stems.

Place four dots of green icing at equal intervals and at the same distance from the edge.

Divide each quarter of the circle into thirds. Place two dots at equal intervals in each quarter and at the same distance from the edge.

Using the method described in *DC*, pp. 62ff., drop No. 1 green stem in zigzag fashion to connect twelve dots. In hollow portions of main stems draw No. 1 small stems.

Place large flowers on main dots of twelve-point wreath. Add buds, small flowers, or leaves to small stems. Add leaf pattern to large and small stems.

Notice that a twelve-point wreath is rounder than an eight-point.

SIX-POINT WREATH

To make the six-point wreath, first make two No. 2 green dots opposite each other and at the same distance from the edge. (Fig. 7.)

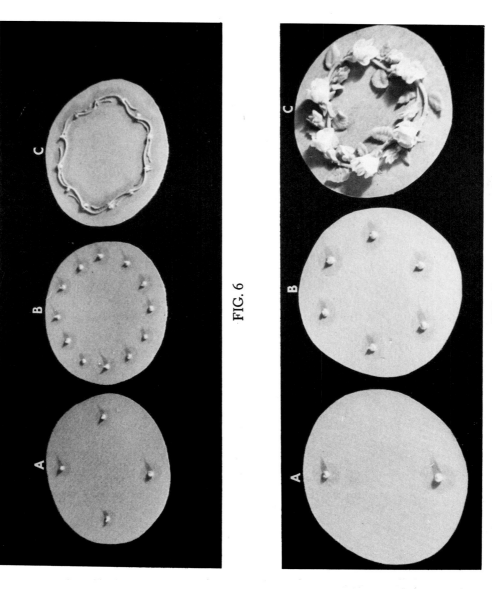

FIG. 6

FIG. 7

Divide each half into thirds. Place in each half two dots at equal intervals and at the same distance from the edge.

Drop No. 1 green stem in zigzag fashion to connect six dots. In hollow portions of main stems draw small stems.

In Fig. 7 3D roses made with a No. 101 white cone were formed on the six main dots. Small rosebuds were added to small stems. Appropriate greenery was added. The six-point wreath is good for a small round, triangular, or heart-shaped cake.

TEN-POINT WREATH

Place five dots of green icing at equal intervals and at the same distance from the edge of the cardboard. (Fig. 8.)

Place dots of green icing between the original five.

Drop No. 1 green stem in zigzag fashion to connect ten dots. In hollow portions of main stems, draw No. 1 small stems.

Place large flowers on main dots. Add buds, small flowers, or leaves to small stems. Add leaf pattern to large and small stems.

The ten-point wreath is very round and graceful.

WREATH FOR SQUARE CAKE

To make a wreath for a square cake, first make a pencil pattern by drawing the main stems of an eight-point wreath against a round cardboard. Then cut out the pattern. (Fig. 9.)

Place the pattern on top of a square cake after the icing is crusted slightly. Press the edges of the pattern very lightly to leave an impression in the icing. Remove the pattern.

Drop the main stems on the outline left in the icing. Draw the small stems. Add flowers (No. 101s) and leaves.

If you wish, place a rose or small corsage in each corner of the cake.

In any case, the wreath will fit the square cake, and it will also be graceful and pleasing.

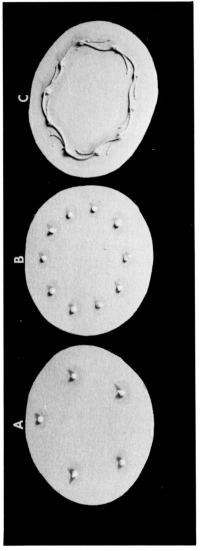

FIG. 8

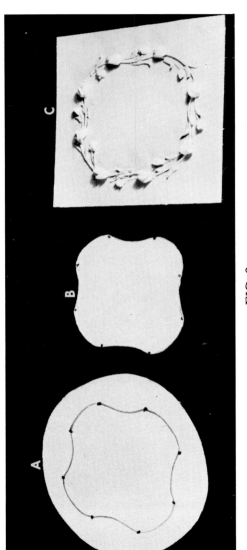

FIG. 9

WREATH FOR RECTANGULAR CAKE

Use the same fundamental point system. The cardboard models for this lesson are 3¼ inches by 5 inches. (Fig. 10.)

Place a No. 2 green dot at the middle of each side and three-eighths of an inch inside each edge.

With ruler or pencil measure from a corner to a point midway between two dots. Then move point out from center so that it will form part of an oval shape. Make a dot of green icing at this final point.

Measure the distance from corner to the last green dot. Measure the same distance from the other three corners and make dots of green icing to form an oval shape.

Eight points will make a "lopsided" rectangular wreath. A twelve-point wreath will be perfectly oval in shape. The latter can be made by dividing each quarter into thirds and measuring twice from each corner.

As you can see in the illustration, a sixteen-point wreath makes a smooth oval pattern. This is easily accomplished by placing eight more dots between the original eight. (A similar technique can be used for an oval-shaped cake.)

Using the same technique as in previous wreaths, drop No. 2 stems in an even zigzag fashion that joins the sixteen points. Then, starting at each main point, draw a smaller stem that fills in a hollow portion of the main stem.

Using a No. 101s pink cone, make sweet peas on main points, pointing them in the direction the main stem is going. Make sweet pea buds on small stems.

Use No. 2 green cone to make sepals and pressure leaves. Use No. 101s pink cone for nail rose in corners. Make ⅛-inch V-cone green rose leaves. Form lettering with No. 2 green cone.

The cakes you decorate may be 9 inches by 13 inches, or half-sheets, or full-sized baker sheets. The latter are often used as centerpieces for the speakers' tables at banquets. They are propped up on one side in order to display properly the message written or printed within the large oval wreath.

Use any flowers you choose on wreaths that you make. Try roses on main points; on the small stems use rosebuds, just leaves, or small flowers such as forget-me-nots, lilies of the valley, or fantasy flowers. At Christmastime use poinsettias on main points and holly on small stems. There is no limit to the possible variations.

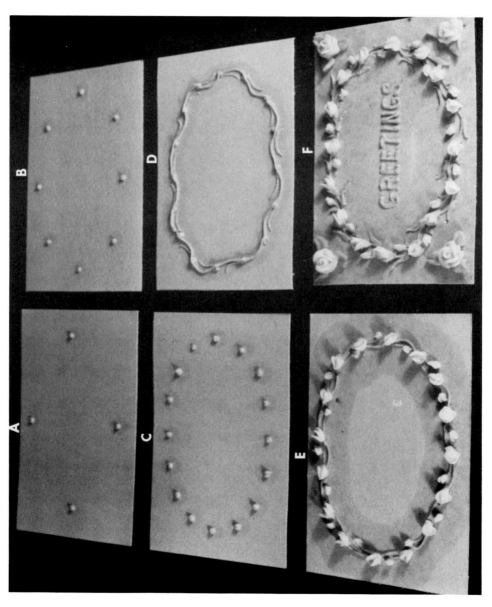

FIG. 10

CORSAGE DESIGN

This corsage design can be used for many flowers, including roses and apple blossoms on the sides of shower and wedding cakes. (Fig. 11.)

Take a 5-inch length of florist wire or similar soft wire. Bend it into a shallow double curve (S curve), and then bend both ends upward to form handles.

After the icing on the cake has crusted a little, make a slight impression with wire at regular intervals around the side of the cake. Have the wire cross over the center of the first impression in each design and make the impressions for the second and third stems. (The use of a wire template will secure a more uniform design when it is repeated.)

Draw No. 3 green icing against impressions, but lengthen center stems at both ends.

Using No. 125 green icing and pivoting the base of the tube, make four circular leaves (as pictured) or make tapered leaves with a V-cone. (Circular leaves can be made separately and then frozen or dried before being placed in arrangement.) Taper circular leaves slightly between thumb and finger before they dry.

Make No. 103 triple-tone, blue violets on ice can or similar frozen surface. When they are frozen, remove them with a cold paring knife and place them on leaves. When petals thaw they will fall into natural position against irregular surface of leaves.

If you need more instruction, please study *BCF*: flower-tube leaves, pp. 48f.; triple-toning, pp. 144f.; violets, pp. 150ff. Notice the variations of the corsage design in 27C, pp. 3 and 12.

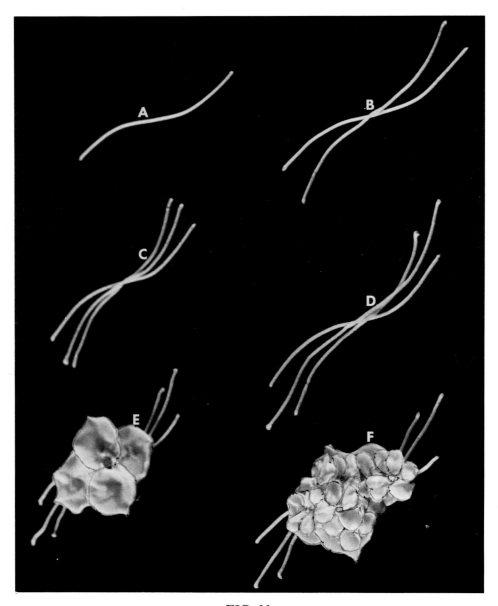

FIG. 11

IV

FIGURE PIPING

BEADING AND ROPING

Beading and roping are involved in the art of figure piping. It is just as well to practice them first.

The top row of Fig. 12 was formed with a small No. 4 cone of very *soft* buttercream icing. The rest of the illustration was formed with a No. 3 cone. Royal icing can be used in the same way. All of the techniques can produce much smaller or much larger work, depending upon the size of the tube that is used.

The work in miniature is used on sugar cubes or mints, or it can be made larger with pastry tubes on wedding cakes. The techniques are often used in lettering, as illustrated in the bottom row. Back-away beads (at the right) also make excellent bamboo and fine furniture. Roping is appropriate in basket making.

Many special uses will be found for beading and roping. Most of the time they border petit fours, pastries, and cakes. Sometimes they finish the edges of royal-icing work, gum-paste creations or ornamental pieces, or sugar pieces.

Using a No. 4 small cone of *very soft* white buttercream icing, practice the first row of shell beads at the upper left. Hold the cone at a 45-degree angle. Make the same loop motion as for shell work. Gradually increase pressure and then gradually decrease pressure.

After you have successfully made shell beads, then make continuous beads as illustrated in the second row. Don't quite stop the pressure or touch the surface. These are faster and very useful in finishing latticed work.

Shell beads and continuous beads are shown in horizontal rows also.

The third vertical row from the left is "rope." Holding the cone at a 45-degree angle, and slanting it so that it is leading the rope, make a small circular motion and bring cone toward you.

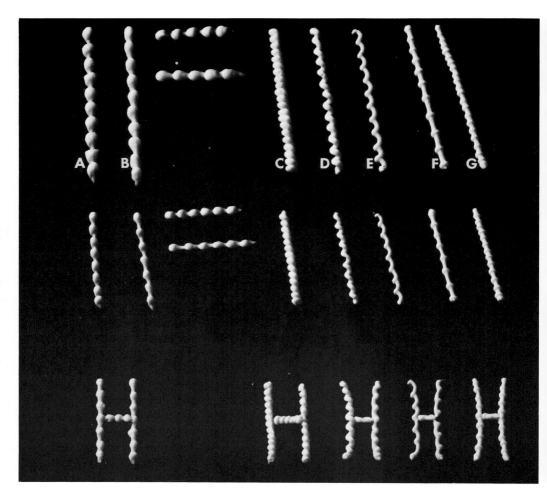

FIG. 12

The fourth vertical row from the left is "stretched rope." Bring cone toward you faster, but make the rope at the same rate of speed.

The fifth vertical row from the left is "modified rope." Do not lift the tube off the surface as you pretend to make stretched rope.

The sixth and seventh rows from the left are "back-away beads." Keep cone at a 45-degree angle and touching the surface. Keep pressure on icing steady. Move tube toward you; stop; move tube toward you; stop; etc. The tube was moved a longer distance each time in row six than in row seven. This technique is easy and it's fun.

The letter *H* is formed with continuous bead, rope, stretched rope, modified rope, and back-away bead. Try them, and then do the rest of the alphabet with various techniques of roping and beading.

CORNUCOPIAS

Cornucopias, or horns of plenty, are common symbols of the harvest season. In recent times we not only fill them with miniature marzipan fruits and vegetables, but with flowers as well. Even wedding cakes are sometimes decorated with cornucopias of flowers.

Horns of plenty can be molded of sugar, but it is also helpful to be able to figure pipe them directly on a pastry or cake or on absorbent paper for drying and later use. They can be made small enough for French pastries or large enough for buffet centerpieces.

Bend a piece of wire into the shape of the first part of Fig. 13; then bend both ends of wire upward to form handles. Press the wire lightly into crusted icing on cake to leave a slight impression. Then change position of wire and make second impression near first one, as in the second part of Fig. 13. This not only helps guide the decorator later, but it also is a way to secure greater uniformity when the same design is repeated.

Do not put down lines of icing as in Fig. 13 because the icing will be in the way of the roping. The lines of icing in the illustration are for instructional purposes only. Just make an impression in the icing or put down a pattern in some other way.

In the second row make two impressions with a smaller wire. Then hold a No. 5 cone of soft white icing at a 45-degree angle and start roping between the lines. Notice that as the horn becomes wider, more pressure is exerted on the icing and the rope becomes thicker. At the last stage gradually use a lower angle (point tube downward more) and pile the rope so that it forms a hollow space.

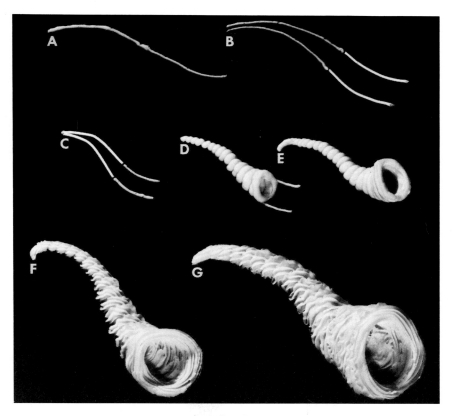

FIG. 13

Repeat the same technique with No. 27 star cone and No. 30 star cone as in the third row of Fig. 13.

The work in the illustration was done with buttercream icing, but it can also be done with royal icing, boiled icing, or meringue torte.

GRAPE DESIGN

The grape design was done with very *soft* buttercream icing. Royal icing can be used also. (Fig. 14.)

This design is a very ancient one, with great traditional significance. When done in white on the side of a wedding cake, it has dignity and appropriateness hard to match.

In color it is very good during the harvest season and especially for Thanksgiving Day. It can be used on top or side of cake.

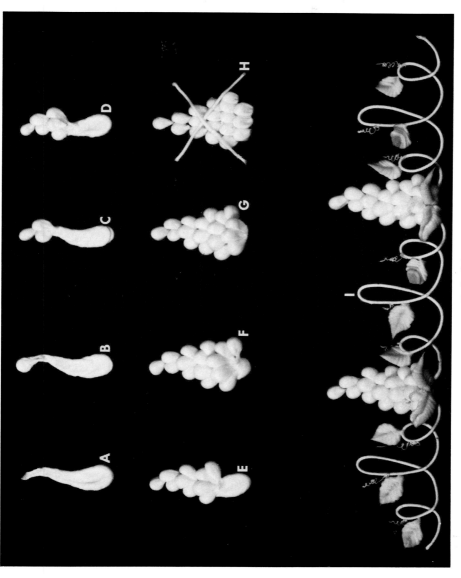

FIG. 14

The bunches of buttercream grapes can be made on absorbent paper towel and allowed to dry overnight. Then they can be fastened to the side of the cake with fresh icing. This is easier for most students, although some will want to make them directly on the cake when they become expert.

The illustration will seem upside down to you. This is for instructional purposes. If you want to see how the grape design looks when it's on the cake, turn the page around.

Practice with a No. 5 cone of very *soft* white icing. Make an S-shaped mound of icing that is large at the bottom and small at the top.

Make a bead (like a shell) that is high and short.

Add rows two and three so that they just touch each other. Point tube from center to left, to center, and to right when making grapes. Avoid making straight lines. The scheme used here is one, two, three, four, five, three, but you can make up a different one if you wish.

The illustration with an X through it shows what *not* to do. Do *not* make straight rows. Do *not* point all grapes straight ahead.

The e-l-e stem design is made with a No. 3 green cone and drop technique; the tendrils, with a very fine paper cone of green icing; and the leaves, with a ⅜-inch V-cone of green icing.

FIGURE PIPING

Figure piping is often a combination of drawing and bulb technique. You do not have to be skillful or talented to follow the simple lines of the step-by-step illustrations in Figs. 17 and 18. However, when you need to give depth to parts of the rabbit or cat or any other figure piping, you must understand and use bulb technique.

When practicing bulb technique, use a small, plain paper cone with a small, round opening at the end, or use a metal tube with a plain, round opening. The icing must be very *soft*, softer than it would be for leaves and stems.

Hold the cone at a 45-degree angle to the surface against which you are working. Start with a light pressure. As soon as the icing is fastened well to the surface, push the rim of the cone or tube opening below the surface of the icing already placed, and keep it below the surface.

Gradually increase pressure as you slowly lift tube *straight* up from the surface against which you are working (but keep the tube opening *below* the surface of the icing). When the ball of icing is the size you wish, stop pressure and remove the tube *from the side* of the ball. (It is somewhat like pumping air into a balloon.)

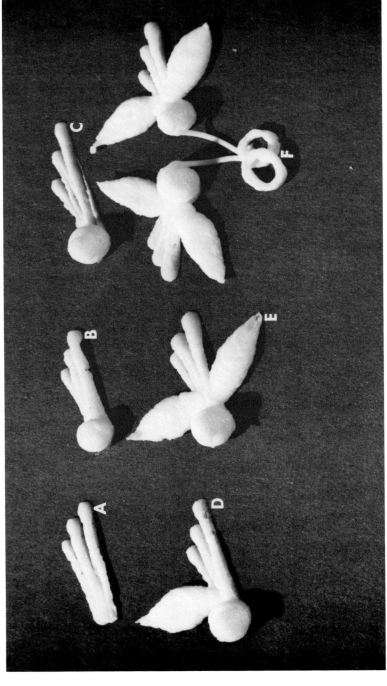

FIG. 15

LOVEBIRDS

When you learn to figure pipe birds with buttercream or royal icing, they can be made of the same material as the other decorations. This gives an effect of greater dignity and restraint, especially on wedding cakes. You can also make certain that the size of the birds is appropriate to the size of the cake.

The type of bird in Fig. 15 can be used equally well on the top of a cake. (Illustration from *DC*, p. 85.) Two birds may be placed close together, with or without the double-ring motif. Many other ideas for bird designs can be gained from a study of cards, wrappings, and paper napkins and tablecloths.

In order to secure greater uniformity where the lovebird motif is repeated, press a marker lightly against the icing before beginning the figure piping. Form the marker from florist or other light wire into a wide V shape. Then bend the top ends toward you to form the handles. Bend the bottom of the V toward you so that it will not leave an indentation on the cake. The two separated, diagonal lines that the marker leaves on the cake will represent the first stroke of the tail structure for each bird.

Use a No. 3 tube in a *small* cone of *very soft* icing.

Hold the tube close to the cake and slanted to the right.

Run the lines with constant pressure, from left to right to left, three times. Separate lines slightly at the right, but always bring them to the same starting point at the left. Make each line longer than the one above it.

Tilt cone toward you and gradually lift it as you make a ball of icing at the left. You may wish to finish the body by reducing pressure and bringing the tube into the tail structure.

Tilt cone toward you and place tube inside upper third of body. Start pressure and gradually bring bulb of icing out of body. Stop pressure and flick tube to left to form beak.

Hold tube in vertical position at back of bird's body. Gradually increasing pressure and lifting tube, and gradually decreasing pressure and lowering tube, form right wing at right angle to tail.

In a similar way form left wing at angle parallel to end of tail.

For a second type of figure-piped bird (Fig. 16) continue to use *very soft* buttercream icing or royal icing and a small cone with a No. 3 tube. Birds may be piped directly against a cake. However, if you wish to dry them for later use, pipe buttercream against absorbent paper (such as paper towel), and pipe royal icing against waxed paper.

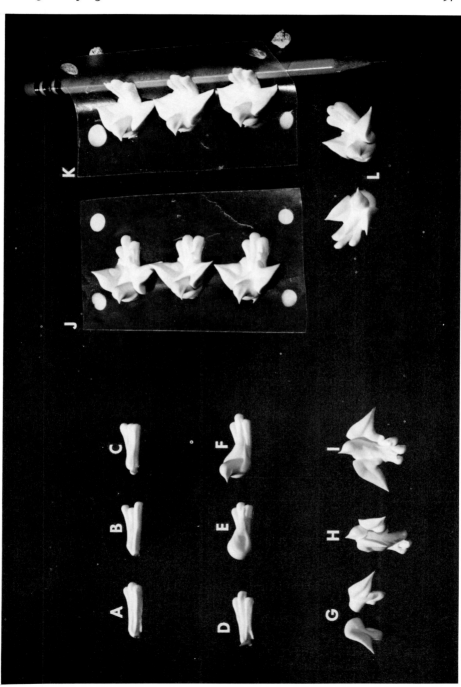

FIG. 16

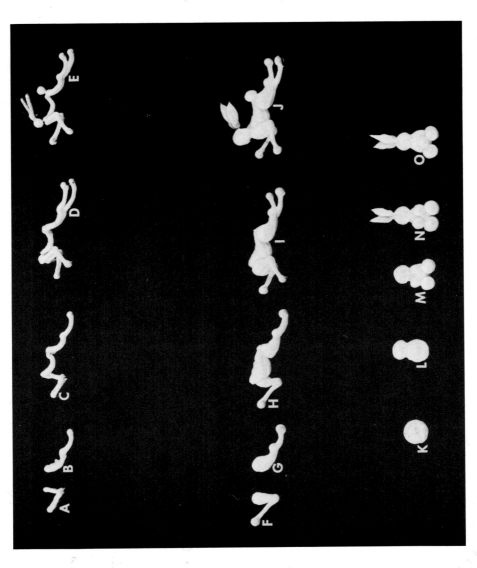

FIG. 17

Holding the cone at a 45-degree angle and lightly against the surface, exert a light, steady pressure and move tube to right and left, to right and left, to right and left. Each time the tube goes to the right, make the tail wider, but each time the tube goes to the left, keep the tail narrow. (Notice the different shapes the end of the tail may take, depending upon how long the center right stroke is.)

In the second step of the second row, holding the cone at a 45-degree angle, place the tube opening at the left end of the tail, exert pressure and lift slightly to make a round body; then reduce pressure gradually as you bring tube down and to the right.

In step three of the second row, holding cone at a 45-degree angle, place tube opening in the *side* of the body, start pressure, and lift tube up and out of body to form head. *Stop pressure.* Move tube abruptly to left to form beak.

The first example in row three shows a different way of making wings. Make a ¼-inch paper V-cone of icing (as for leaf work).

Holding paper cone on edge and at a 45-degree angle exert a steady pressure; after a base is formed, lift cone up, and then forward, and then back, gradually bringing pressure to a halt to form point of wing.

In the second example of row three, the wings are made close against the body. In the third example the wings are opened wide. The latter is accomplished by tilting the cone to the right or to the left when the wings are being formed.

When birds are perched, the tails often slant upward. To achieve this effect, make a row of birds on paper. Then place a pencil under the paper in such a way that the tails are hiked upward. Let them dry for 24 hours before removing them from the paper.

EASTER RABBITS

The work in Fig. 17 was done with very soft buttercream decorating icing (pp. 191-192). It can also be done equally well with royal icing. A No. 3 tube was used.

Figure piping, as explained previously, is a combination of drawing and bulb technique. That is why the first row in the illustration is a step-by-step stick drawing.

The first front leg is a left-handed check mark, and the first back leg is a very slender, lazy, written *E*, lying on its back.

The body is a shallow letter *U*.

The second front leg is another check mark, made slightly to the right of the first front leg and bent close to the body.

The second back leg is another slender, written *E*, made on top of the first one, but raised slightly higher.

The head, ears, and tail are self-explanatory.

After practicing the stick drawing, try doing the second row, putting flesh on the bones by using very soft icing and bulb technique. The latter is accomplished by holding the cone at a 45-degree angle to the surface, by increasing pressure and lifting the tube opening away from the surface, and by decreasing pressure and lowering the tube opening toward the surface. Most pressure is exerted where the legs or body is thickest, least pressure where the legs are thinnest.

To make the rabbit's head, increase pressure and lift tube to form a ball of icing. Stop pressure and move tube to left or right to avoid leaving a point of icing. (Form powder-puff tail in the same way.)

To form each ear, hold the tube straight down and slightly off the surface. Then move tube to right, gradually increasing and then decreasing pressure.

In the third row a different and easier rabbit is illustrated. Hold the cone straight down and just off the surface. Make a "yo-yo"-shaped round spot of icing. Stop pressure and lift cone.

Make a second, smaller spot of icing above the first one.

Form two large dots of icing at the base of the first "yo-yo," and then form two smaller dots that are above the first two, but not as far apart.

Make rabbit ears just like those described for the running rabbit.

Add features with brush or icing. Show rabbit eating a carrot, if you wish.

In the last illustration omit two small dots and make a powder-puff tail instead. Then you get a different view of the bunny.

HALLOWEEN CATS

The first row in Fig. 18 is a step-by-step stick drawing.

The first front leg is a check mark and the first back leg is a very slender, written *E*.

The body is a letter *U*, upside down.

The second front leg is a check mark, lengthened and brought downward.

The second back leg is another slender, written *E* that crosses over and to the left of the first back leg.

The head and tail are self-explanatory.

After practicing the stick drawing, try doing the second row, putting

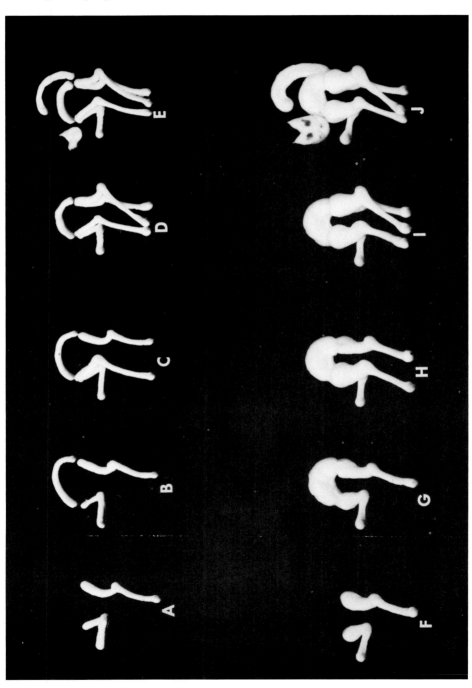

FIG. 18

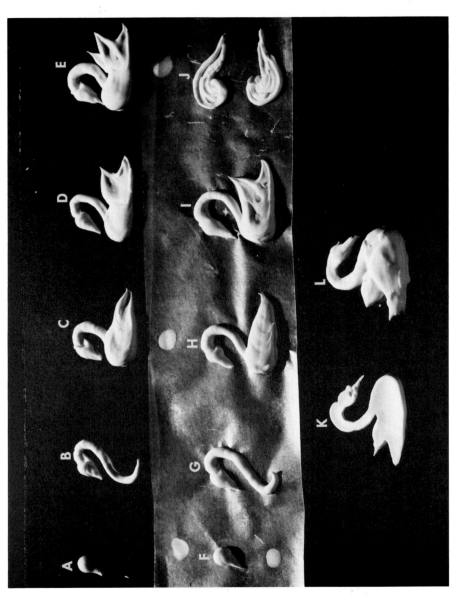

FIG. 19

flesh on the bones by using very soft icing and the bulb technique. The latter is accomplished by holding the cone at a 45-degree angle to the surface, by increasing pressure and lifting the tube opening away from the surface, and by decreasing pressure and lowering the tube opening toward the surface. Most pressure is exerted where the legs or body is thickest, least pressure where the legs are thinnest.

To make the cat's head, increase pressure and lift tube to form a ball of icing. To form each ear, push tube into top edge of head; then bring tube out of head quickly. Use a slight pressure if necessary. Color eyes, mouth, and whiskers with brush and vegetable color or with colored icing.

These cats, done in black, will look very Halloweenish as they stand on a back fence or on the end of a broom.

SWANS

Swans are appropriate for wedding and bridal shower cakes. They may be figure piped directly on the side of a cake with very soft buttercream icing or royal icing. They may also be made separately, dried, and then fastened to the cake with fresh icing.

The first row in Fig. 19 shows how swans may be figured piped directly against the cake.

Using either buttercream or royal icing and holding a No. 3 small cone at a 45-degree angle, make a carrot-shaped object for the head and beak. Fasten an S-shaped neck at the top of the head.

Holding the tube at a right angle to the surface and off the surface, increase pressure until body is formed; then move tube to right to form tail, gradually reducing pressure and lowering tube to the surface.

To form wing, hold cone at a right angle to the surface, place tube below surface of body, start pressure, move tube upward and to the right while gradually reducing pressure. If you wish, indicate a second wing in a similar manner.

When royal icing is used to form a three-dimensional swan, use the same method through the fourth step in the second row, but make the swans against waxed paper. When they have dried thoroughly (24 hours or more), take them off the waxed paper and turn them upside down (left figure in third row).

Figure pipe head, neck, body, and wing on top of dried half (right figure in third row). When swans are dry on both sides, stand them upright on some fresh icing.

A variation on this method is to stop with the third step in the second row. Then make wings separately as in step five. When wingless swan is dried and figure piped as in third row, let it dry a second time, stand it upright in fresh icing, and fasten wings to the body with fresh icing.

V

BITS AND PIECES

RIBBONS AND BOWS

Ribbons and bows are used widely on holiday cakes. They are also very appropriate as shower, wedding, anniversary, and birthday decorations. Bows are beautiful in themselves, but they can also be used effectively with bouquets, baskets, corsages, hats, or bells.

A No. 4 cone of soft buttercream icing is used for the first two rows of Fig. 20. A No. 103 cone is used for the third row.

Hold the cone at a medium angle and medium right tilt. Bring the cone up, to the right, and around to the center of the bow; and then up, to the left, and around to the center; and then down to the right.

Notice that the curve can start near the horizontal and finish near the vertical (step two); begin and end near the vertical (step three); begin near the vertical and finish near the horizontal (step four). The fifth step is crossed out to indicate that two curves near the horizontal are not attractive.

In the second row the first step indicates that round bows are more attractive than the flat ones in step two. Step three illustrates a round bow. Step four shows a more formal bow. In steps three and four dots of icing are added to the centers to indicate knots.

Any size flower tube from No. 101s to No. 127 may be used when a three-dimensional effect is desired. In the third row, a No. 103 cone is used at a medium angle and a medium right tilt. (Do *not* change tilt when forming left side of bow or it will collapse.)

Steps one, two, and three correspond to steps two, three, and four in first row. Notice that knots are added to centers of steps three and four by holding tube vertically and moving tube from top to bottom of center area.

After ribbons have dried a few minutes, clip Vs out of ends of ribbons with scissors, as in steps three and four.

FIG. 20

BUTTERCREAM DIPLOMAS

Buttercream is a very practical material for diplomas because it is usually on hand, it is very easy to handle, and it doesn't require drying time.

Thicken buttercream icing with sifted powdered sugar until it handles like modeling clay. Dust a board with cornstarch. Roll thickened icing out evenly to ⅛-inch thickness with a rolling pin. Cut a 4-inch by 5-inch rectangle. (Fig. 21.)

Roll it up so that it is 5 inches long. Press the center together slightly. Pinch edges at both ends and at the front so that they are thinner than the rest of the icing. Touch all edges with brush and golden yellow vegetable color.

With a No. 104 cone of golden yellow soft buttercream icing, make a band of ribbon at the center of the diploma. Then make a bow at the center with the same cone.

If you need help in making bows, please study p. 45.

MAKING FLAGS

Figure 22 represents a method of making a buttercream flag directly on a cake.

A similar flag can be made on waxed paper over a picture or pattern. If very soft royal icing is used, let it dry for 24 hours or more before removing it from the paper. If buttercream is used, freeze it for five minutes, turn flag over, place it on cake, and remove paper. Then add stars to blue field.

Make one cardboard pattern 2 inches by 3 inches. Make a second pattern 1⅜ inches by 1 1/16 inches.

When the icing on the cake is no longer sticky, press large pattern first and then press small one inside the impression made by the large one.

Using a soft red No. 5 cone, and holding the cone almost straight down, make a stripe at top, bottom, and center (from lower right corner of blue field). Space two more red stripes evenly between top and center. Space two more evenly between center and bottom.

Insert soft white No. 5 cone stripes between red ones.

Smooth a thin layer of blue icing on waxed paper. Freeze for three or four minutes. Put small pattern on top of frozen icing and cut around it.

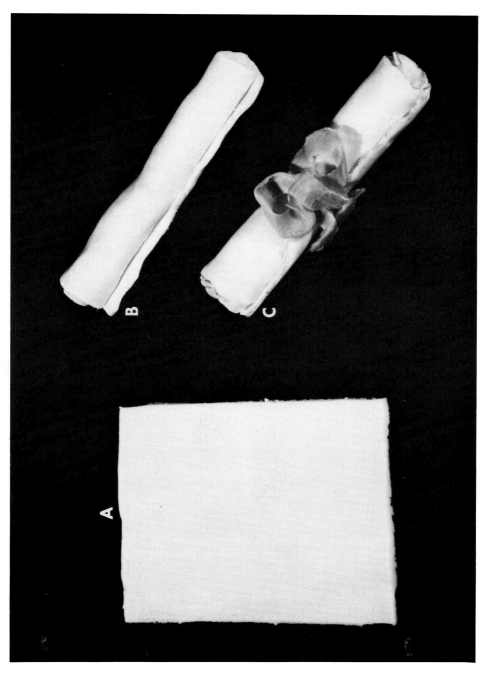

FIG. 21

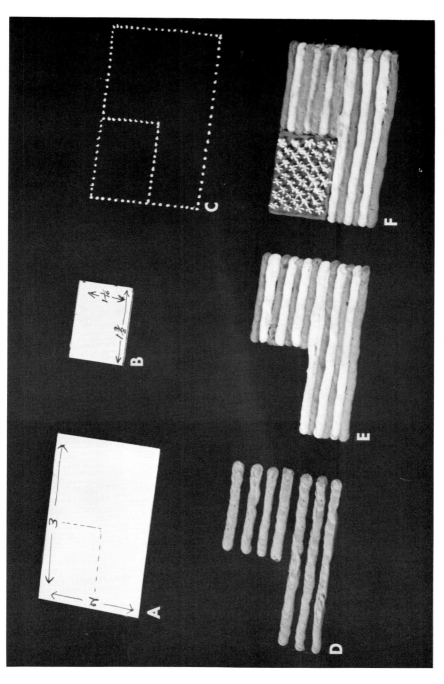

FIG. 22

Cut away excess icing. Put blue field upside down in flag. Peel away and remove waxed paper.

Use light pressure on a white No. 13 cone to make stars. Evenly space six stars across top, bottom, and center. Put one more row of six stars between top and center, and one more row of six stars between center and bottom.

Then mismatch (between the five rows of six stars each) four rows of five stars each.

BUTTERCREAM LATTICED EFFECTS

Ornamental work made with gum-paste pieces and royal-icing latticed pieces changes the contour of a cake. It minimizes angles and makes for a smooth transition from one plane to another.

We have done similar things with buttercream.

Following the steps in Fig. 23, make a column of shells with a No. 30 white cone. Make shells with a low loop, narrow at the top of the column and wider toward the base.

For the second column repeat the work in the first. Then add a second layer of flat, low-loop shells, not as wide as the first layer; start the second layer one shell below the beginning of the first layer.

If you want the column to come out from the side of the cake still more, follow the third example. To column two add a third layer of flat shells, not as wide as the second layer; start the third layer one shell below the beginning of the second layer. Finish the base with a star.

The columns, or pillars, can be used on round cakes of any size. It may be necessary to change the tube size. Use six or more columns. Do not use less than six; otherwise, the smooth transitional effect between base and side will be lost when the cake is viewed from the side.

The last column to the right and on the corner suggests how easily this idea can be adapted to the corners of square or rectangular cakes. In this case vertical and horizontal rows of No. 27 stars were added to the shell column.

FIG. 23

The columns can be made in a similar way with star work or beadwork.

Following the steps in Fig. 24, make one curved design with No. 27 white shells against the side and another curved design against the base. Fill in space between curved lines of shells with a mound of icing from same tube.

In the second step place a large No. 27 star in the center; add stars that become gradually smaller toward each end of the design.

In actual use you may choose to alternate a space of shell work between each of these designs.

The various types of drapery shown in illustrations may be studied in detail in *DC*, pp. 78f.

FIGURE-PIPED BELLS

Bells are appropriate for Christmas and New Year's Day celebrations, as well as for showers, weddings, anniversaries, and certain religious occasions. Sugar bells are excellent, but many decorators overlook the importance of using figure-piped bells when they are more suitable.

If you have many individual pieces of cake to do, bend a small piece of florist wire into the shape of the second item in the first row of Fig. 25. Bend the ends of the wire upward to form two handles.

When the icing on the cakes is crusted slightly, press the wire on the icing just enough to leave a bell outline. Make two impressions on each cake if you wish. In this way you gain uniformity. The design can be imprinted similarly on the top or side of a layer or tiered cake.

The illustrations in Fig. 25 are done freehand. One of the advantages of the figure-piping method is that bells can be custom made, any shape or size. They can also be made as flat or as thick as you wish.

Using a *very soft* No. 5 small cone of buttercream icing, bring a double-curved line from top center to left to bottom of bell. (Royal icing can also be used in the same way.)

Bring a similar line from top to right to bottom of bell.

Make curved line at bottom.

Add ball of icing to base.

Add ribbon to single- or double-bell design by pressing tube straight down into icing and moving tube in zigzag fashion. Put a dot of icing at top of each bell. (The ribbon may also be formed with No. 101 or No. 102 tube.)

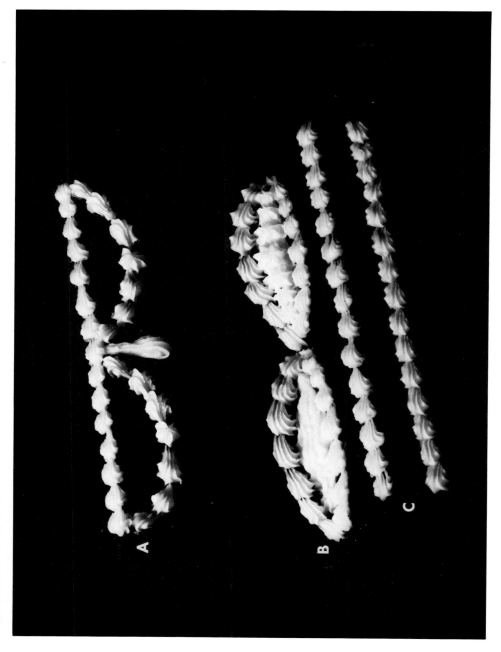

FIG. 24

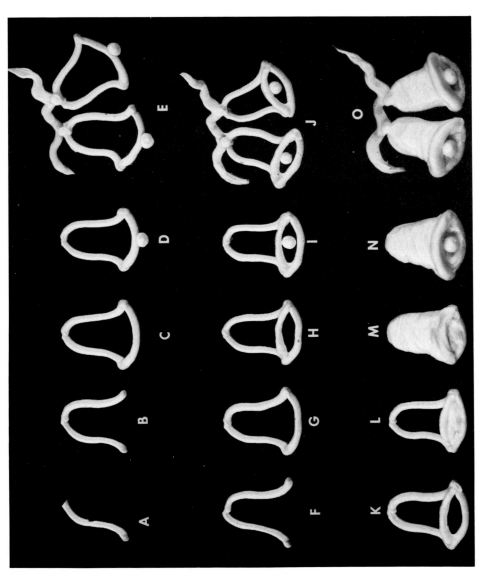

FIG. 25

In row two repeat steps in row one, and add second curved line at base of bell. Put ball of icing between the two curved lines.

In row three repeat steps in row two. Holding cone at a 45-degree angle, move tube left and right and fill in space between the two curved lines at base.

Starting at top and moving tube left and right and left, etc., and keeping tube opening beneath surface of icing, gradually lift tube from surface and increase pressure as the tube is brought down toward the *top* curved line at the bottom. This will cause the bell to become thicker toward the base.

Overpipe the top curved baseline twice to form the bell rim. Add a ball of icing by increasing pressure as the tube is lifted slightly from the surface; stop pressure and move tube left or right to leave a smooth surface.

VI

CREATIONS FOR CHRISTMAS AND NEW YEAR'S

HOLIDAY CAKE

Ice 10-inch round cake and 12-inch baseboard with light blue icing. (Fig. 26, p. 65.) Using a brush and liquid vegetable colors, shade the center top area irregularly with light green and gold.

Make evergreen with *very fine* paper cone and *very soft* green icing.

Make brown-gold bells with *very soft* icing and No. 4 cone. Smooth surfaces with damp brush. Decorate bells with dark brown icing and No. 1 cone. Make rope for bells with No. 2 dark brown cone.

Use No. 3 *very soft* white cone for bodies, heads, and tails of birds. Use regular consistency of white icing for 5/16-inch V-cone to make wings. Overpipe wings with *very soft, very fine* cone of white icing to indicate feathers.

Make more evergreen on top of bells. Use *very fine* paper cone of very soft green icing.

Form scroll pattern at intervals on side of cake with No. 2 cone of soft brown-gold icing.

Print *Season's Greetings* in English, French, and Spanish on baseboard. Use No. 1 cone of *very soft*, brown-gold icing.

Make rope border at top with No. 5 light blue cone. Make outside base border rope with No. 3 light blue cone.

If you need further help, please study the following: roping, p. 29; birds, p. 36.

CHRISTMAS QUILT

Ice top and sides of 10-inch by 6½-inch layer cake with Christmas red icing. (Fig. 27, p. 66; also frontispiece.) If you prefer, ice the cake white and decorate with red designs.

Mark design of squares into top and sides of cake with edge of ruler or knife.

Fold waxed or parchment paper and cut pattern for tree. Unfold pattern and lay it on top of cake. Mark around pattern with a sharp knife. Remove pattern.

Place cake in freezer for ten minutes. Remove red icing within area marked by tree pattern and cut with knife.

Spread thin layer of green icing on waxed paper and freeze for five minutes. Place tree pattern on frozen green icing and cut away excess icing. With paper side up, place green icing tree in empty space on top of cake. Peel the paper away from the icing.

Use similar technique to make white disc at top of tree that will become background for small poinsettia.

Decorate squares with simple white icing designs as in Fig. 27, or with other designs that you dream up. Use Nos. 13, 2, and 1 cones as necessary.

Decorate Christmas tree with No. 3 green cone and modified rope. Add red balls with a No. 2 cone on top of the green roping, and small red lines below the green roping. Border the tree with No. 3 modified green rope.

Use No. 2 green cone and stretched rope to sew squares together.

Put No. 101 white rickrack (zigzag) around bottom edge of quilt.

If you need further help, please study roping, p. 29, poinsettias, DC, p. 43; imaginative flowers, DC, pp. 26f. and pp. 38f.; rickrack, DC, p. 99.

SEASON'S GREETINGS

Cover a 10-inch layer cake and a 12-inch baseboard with white icing. (Fig. 28, p. 67.)

Cut three different paper patterns to represent Christmas tree ornaments. Press paper patterns into white icing and then remove them.

Press a plastic snowflake ornament into the crusted white icing at five places. (The blue snowflake in the lower left is more nearly like the original plastic snowflake ornament. You may make up a pattern of your own.)

Fill areas imprinted for the three ornaments with very *soft* lavender, Christmas red, and blue buttercream icings. Mound icing at the center of each ornament and then smooth surface with a moist brush.

Drop fine threads of black icing from top edge of cake down to tops of ornaments.

With No. 3 cones of very *soft* lavender, Christmas red, and blue buttercream icing fill in snowflake patterns in the white icing where they are not covered by the other ornaments.

Change the pattern of each snowflake even though the plastic pattern, or your original pattern, may have been the same when the imprints were made.

Use a modified rope technique and a No. 27 cone of white icing for top border.

Print SEASON'S GREETINGS in different languages and colors around baseboard. Finish inside and outside base borders with No. 13 white shells.

If you need help, please study roping, p. 29; shell work, *DC*, pp. 72ff.

A HOLIDAY CUSTOM

Bevel the top edge of a three-layer, 10-inch round cake. (Fig. 29, p. 68.) Cover the cake and edge of 12-inch baseboard with white icing.

Draw patterns of deer on parchment paper. Cut out patterns and press them lightly against crusted white icing. Remove patterns.

Make a thin, ⅛-inch layer of golden brown buttercream icing on waxed paper. Freeze for five minutes. Place patterns on surface of frozen brown icing and cut away excess icing with a sharp, thin knife. Remove patterns.

Place brown icing deer in freezer for five minutes. Then remove frozen deer from waxed paper and place them on top of cake where patterns made an impression in the white icing.

Using a No. 2 cone of golden brown icing, make horns on boy deer and holly leaves on head of girl deer.

Using a No. 1 cone of black icing, make a bow tie on boy deer and a necklace on girl deer. Put eyes and noses on both.

Make gray-brown trunks of large pine trees with a No. 5 plain paper cone opening. Make upper branches with medium green icing and a ¼-inch V-cone. Use ⅜-inch V-cone for lower branches.

Hang a small branch of mistletoe just above the deer. Use a very fine paper cone opening and black icing to make string that is fastened to tops of trees, forms a bow knot, then travels down to mistletoe, where it is fastened securely with another bow knot.

Make mistletoe with No. 2 green stems, green ⅛-inch V-cone leaves, and No. 2 cream-white berries. Dot each berry with a pin that has been touched to black vegetable color.

Make five small trees on front side of cake with No. 3 cone of gray-brown icing and ¼-inch V-cone of green icing. Add No. 3 round red ornaments to the first, third, and fifth trees; add cream-white ones to the second and fourth trees.

Using clear piping gel, make No. 2 alternate beadwork at the outside base border.

If you need further help, please study evergreen trees, p. 18; mistletoe, *BCF*, pp. 64f.

POINSETTIA CANDLE

Cover a 9½-inch by 13-inch cake with light green icing. (Fig. 30, p. 69.)

Cut a paper candle pattern that is 11 inches long, 2 inches in width at the base and 2 inches in width at the top.

Spread soft white buttercream icing about 3/16-inch thick on a sheet of waxed paper. Place it in a freezer for five minutes.

Press paper pattern lightly against crusted icing on top of cake. Remove pattern.

Take frozen white buttercream icing out of freezer and place candle pattern on top of it. Following pattern, cut through frozen icing and waxed paper with a sharp paring knife.

Lift white candle-shaped icing, turn it upside down, and place it against imprinted space on top of cake. Remove waxed paper from top of candle.

Cut a slight hollow from the top of the candle. Using a 3/16-inch V-cone of yellow icing, make a candle flame. Brush the edges and base of flame with red color.

Make centers of poinsettias with small green dots, covered with yellow dots, topped with very small red dots. Using equal parts of soft buttercream icing and piping gel, make red leaves of poinsettias with ⅛-inch V-cone. (The gel and icing mixture has a shiny appearance and it can be cut easily.)

Draw brown stems for holly with No. 3 size paper cone opening.

Make holly leaves with equal parts of soft buttercream icing and piping gel. Use a ¼-inch V-cone. Form points with a moist brush before leaves set up.

Form holly berries with some of the icing mixed for poinsettia leaves. Use a No. 3 cone and bulb technique. Put a very small dot of black on each berry with a pin or very fine brush.

Do borders with the same light green icing used for icing cake. Make continuous bead (and roping below the base of the candle) with a No. 5 cone.

If you need help, please study the following; beading and roping, p. 29; poinsettias, DC, p. 43; holly, BCF, p. 52.

HOLIDAY WELCOME

Trim a layer cake so that it is 11 inches by 6½ inches. (Fig. 31, p. 70.) Round the top. Ice the cake with white icing.

Make three grooves lengthwise with the edge of a spatula. Cover top rounded part of cake with yellow-orange piping gel. Cover small ornamental pieces of dried gum-paste work with yellow-orange piping gel. Place them at the right side of the door to represent a door handle and lock. (See recipe for gum paste on p. 62.)

Cut a circle of parchment paper that is 2¼-inches in diameter. Press it against the crusted white icing of the door. Remove paper pattern.

Mix equal parts of piping gel and buttercream icing. Make medium green holly leaves with a ⅛-inch V-cone into a wreath. Make poinsettias with a ⅛-inch V-cone of red piping gel. Add a few holly berries of red piping gel with a No. 2 cone.

Add a Christmas red buttercream ribbon made with a No. 102 cone.

Using a No. 4 cone of light green icing, drop lines over yellow-orange piping gel above top of door.

With the corrugated side up, use a No. 46 cone of light green icing to make the pillars at each side of the door. (Make two lines for each pillar to get enough width.) Finish the tops with some beadwork with the No. 4 green cone. Flatten top of beadwork with a knife.

Make board below door (two widths smoothed together) and those around sides of cake (single width) with white icing in a No. 46 tube, smooth side up.

If you need help, please study ribbons, p. 45; beading, p. 29; poinsettias, DC, p. 43; holly, BCF, p. 52.

Gum Paste

Dissolve ⅜ ounce granulated gelatin in ½ cup hot water. Add 1½ pounds powdered sugar and 1 ounce cornstarch. Mix until smooth, cover tightly, and let stand overnight. Then work to right consistency (like modeling clay) with powdered sugar and use. Keep unused portion of gum paste covered with damp cloth.

A NEW YEAR'S PRAYER

Place a 10-inch cake on a 12-inch base and cover them with light blue icing. (Fig. 32, p. 63.*)

With brush and liquid vegetable colors add yellow band near top-rear and sides and base; then a green band similarly from base, up side, along top, down opposite side, and along base; then a light blue band of color; then a darker blue band.

Where different colors touch each other, use water on brush and blend colors so that there is a gradual transition.

Make a variety of birds: different sizes, wings in different positions, tails spread differently, flying in different directions. Use very *soft* white buttercream icing and a No. 3 tube. Use a 3/16-inch V-cone for the wings that are raised off the surface.

Pipe letters of message with a No. 3 cone of soft white icing. Overpipe letters with beadwork from the same tube.

Form beadwork at baseboard with No. 3 cone of soft light blue icing.

If you need help in making birds, please study p. 36; beading, p. 29.

HOLIDAY BELL

Use one 2-inch layer or stack two 1-inch layers. (Fig. 33, p. 64.) Cut a bell paper pattern that is 8½ by 9½ inches. Lay pattern on cake; cut around pattern. Remove pattern and bevel top edges except for base of bell.

Do not allow baseboard to project beyond cake. Ice cake white.

With a pin etch main lines of design into the icing when it is dry.

---

*Black-and-white photos appearing after Chapter V also appear in color and can be found by referring to the page number following the figure number of the corresponding black-and-white photo. The letter C indicates a color cross-reference.

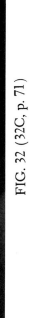

FIG. 32 (32C, p. 71)

FIG. 33 (33C, p. 71)

FIG. 26 (text, p. 57)

FIG. 27 (text, p. 58)

FIG. 28 (text, p. 58)

FIG. 29 (text, p. 59)

FIG. 30 (text, p. 60)

FIG. 31 (text, p. 61)

FIG. 32 (text, p. 62)

FIG. 33 (text, p. 62)

71

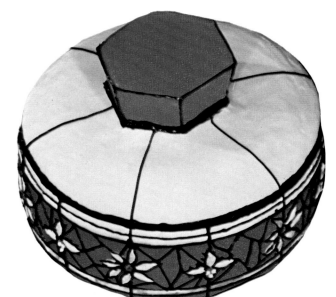

FIG. 34 (text, p. 81)

FIG. 35 (text, p. 83)

FIG. 36 (text, p. 85)

FIG. 37 (text, p. 87)

73

FIG. 38 (text, p. 89)

FIG. 39 (text, p. 89)

FIG. 40 (text, p. 92)

FIG. 41 (text, p. 93)

FIG. 42 (text, p. 95)

FIG. 43 (text, p. 95)

FIG. 44 (text, p. 97)

FIG. 45 (text, p. 98)

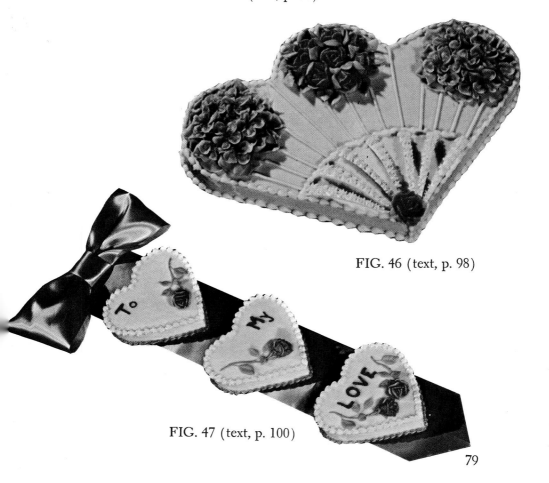

FIG. 46 (text, p. 98)

FIG. 47 (text, p. 100)

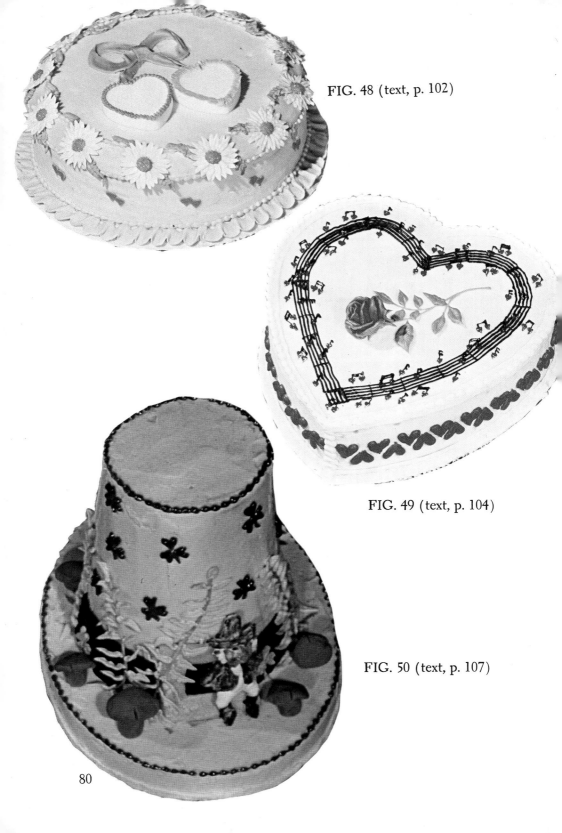

FIG. 48 (text, p. 102)

FIG. 49 (text, p. 104)

FIG. 50 (text, p. 107)

80

Using a No. 3 cone of soft Christmas red buttercream icing, trace over etched lines. Then add more lines to them as necessary. (All decorations except sugar bells and white borders will be Christmas red.)

Add holly leaves with a ¼-inch V-cone. Form points with a brush and water.

Add small tapered leaves with a ⅛-inch V-cone.

Overpipe scroll work with a rotary motion and a No. 3 tube, gradually decreasing the size of the circle and the amount of pressure. Using bulb technique (figure-piping technique), place little curved lines of different-sized round berries.

Make a No. 104 bow of ribbon at the top of the bell and add two long streamers. Use No. 3 tube for red hammers in large sugar bells and No. 2 tube for the ones in small bells. Place bells in arrangement.

Decorate base of cake (and bottom of bell) with No. 4 *very soft* white beadwork.

If you need more help, please study beading, p. 29; ribbons, p. 45; figure-piping technique, p. 34; sugar bells, DC, pp. 89ff.; overpiping, DC, p. 77.

HOLIDAY TIFFANY LAMP CAKE

Trim 10-inch layer cake so that top edge is rounded. (Fig. 34, p. 82.)

Using two or three small layers of cake, form the six-sided top section so that it is 2 inches high. Make each side 2 inches wide at the top and 1½ inches wide at the bottom.

Cover rounded top section of 10-inch cake with white icing. Ice rest of 10-inch cake with a light Christmas red icing. Cover six-sided section with red icing and place it on top of 10-inch cake.

Cut a trench, the width of a No. 46 tube, out of the red icing near the base. Fill in with white icing from smooth side of No. 46 cone.

Take equal parts of buttercream decorating icing and piping gel, mix together, and color black.

Using a No. 3 small cone of black icing gel, figure pipe scalloped border at base. Make horizontal black lines at bottom and at top edges of white base band. Make black line at top edge of red icing; make another just ⅜ inch above it.

Using same No. 3 cone, outline top red section. Bring black line from center baseline of each red top section, across white section, to top of red section at side of cake. Bring black line across white band at base and end it at black scalloped border. Form short black lines between original six short lines.

FIG. 34 (34C, p. 72)

Using black icing gel in a No. 46 cone (smooth side up), form band at base of red hexagon at top of cake. Form a similar band ⅜ inch above last horizontal line made around white top section.

In the center of the main red section, at each of the long vertical lines, form several dots of green. Put yellow dots on the green ones; put red dots on the yellow dots.

Mix one part piping gel and two parts of white buttercream decorating icing. Using ¼-inch V-cone and white piping gel, buttercream icing mixture, make poinsettias around centers.

In the center of red side section, at each of the short vertical lines, make three holly leaves with the same cone. Make three white No. 3 holly berries just below center of each group of leaves.

Using a No. 2 cone of black icing gel, outline each petal, leaf, poinsettia center, and group of berries. Fasten flowers and leaves to long and short vertical lines. Make points on holly leaves with tube or brush.

Then make a very irregular pattern of lines on the rest of the red section.

If possible, display cake on a high stand to make it more nearly resemble a lamp.

If you need help, please study poinsettias, *DC*, p. 43; holly, *BCF*, p. 52.

PARTRIDGE IN A PEAR TREE

Ice 9-inch by 13-inch cake with very light green icing. (Fig. 35, p. 84.)

Using two shades of green in a ¼-inch V-cone, make mistletoe leaves on a wavy No. 3 green stem around the sides of the cake. (Notice that leaves are pear shaped.)

Figure pipe clusters of round mistletoe berries at each set of leaves with a No. 2 cone of *very soft* cream-white icing. Stop pressure before removing tube from each berry, and then move tube gently to one side or the other as you remove it from each berry. (In this way you can avoid leaving points on berries.) Add dots of black or dark brown color to berries with pin or fine brush.

Using some of the same very light green icing that is on the cake itself, make No. 3 beads at the top border and No. 5 beads at the base border and corners.

Fasten waxed paper to a metal surface with a few dots of icing.

Ice the paper with a ⅛-inch layer of white icing, and place it in the freezer.

FIG. 35 (35C, p. 72)

Sketch and cut a large paper pear. Remove iced paper from freezer, place pattern on frozen icing, cut around pattern with a sharp knife, and remove excess icing.

Put pear-shaped icing back in freezer for three or four minutes, take it out of freezer, place it upside down on cake top, and remove paper. Add a white stem to pear with a No. 5 cone. Gently smooth edges of pear with fingers and water.

Make branches of pear tree with soft brown icing and a paper cone opening to give them a rough, "woody" appearance. Make narrow, tapered leaves with a 3/16-inch V-cone. Variegate the icing so that the top surface of leaves will be medium green and the bottom surface will be yellow-green.

Thicken buttercream decorating icing with sifted powdered sugar until it becomes like modeling clay. (Marzipan, fondant, coconut candy, etc., may also be used.)

Form yellow pears by hand and paint them with a light pink vegetable color. Place a whole clove (minus round, berrylike part) into base of each pear.

Form the partridge by hand from thickened white icing and paint with vegetable colors as follows: breast, yellow with black Vs; tail and wings, red; head, black with yellow beak and white eye (with black dot in center). Add a crest to the head with a No. 2 cone of black icing.

Place partridge and pears on tree branches.

If you need help in making mistletoe, please study BCF, p. 64f.

PEACE ON EARTH

Cover a 10-inch cake and a 12-inch baseboard with a light mint-green icing. (Fig. 36, p. 86.)

Thicken a small amount of white buttercream decorating icing with sifted powdered sugar until it is like marzipan. Dust the thickened buttercream on one side with cornstarch and then press the starch-covered surface against a "praying hands" mold. Lift buttercream out of mold, trim the edges of molded buttercream with scissors or knife, smooth the edges with your fingers, brush away excess cornstarch, and then go over surface with damp cloth or brush.

Place buttercream "hands" at center of cake top. Using *very soft* white icing, border the "hands" with No. 3 beads.

Make a 16-point white wreath around the top border. Use ¼-inch V-cone for poinsettias at the main points. Using same V-cone and a brush, make holly leaves on small stems and on large stems between main points.

FIG. 36 (36C, p. 73)

Use white No. 3 stem for white ¼-inch V-cone leaf work at base border.

Using a No. 125 white cone, hold wedge-shaped tube so that large part of tube opening is held against side of cake and small part of tube opening is pointed downward and away from side of cake. Form ribbon along side of cake.

Clip notches out of ribbon ends with scissors. Using a No. 2 cone of medium green icing, print message on ribbon.

Figure pipe white birds near each end of ribbon with a No. 3 cone of very soft icing.

If you need more instruction, please study wreaths, p. 21; birds, p. 36; poinsettia, *DC*, pp. 43f.; holly, *BCF*, p. 62.

YARN DOLLS

Cover a 10-inch cake on a 12-inch base with white icing. (Fig. 37, p. 88.)

Sketch a pattern for yarn dolls on parchment paper. After a crust has formed on cake icing, press pattern lightly against top of cake and then remove it.

Put mounds of soft Christmas red buttercream icing at several places: heads, bodies, hands, and feet. Then make No. 2 lines of the same icing so that they cover the mounds and resemble yarn.

Using a No. 101s golden-yellow cone, make a wavy bonnet for the girl and two rows of frilly ribbon across her skirt.

Tie the yarn at her wrists with a No. 2 red cone.

With a No. 2 cone of golden-yellow icing, make a bow at her throat and make five-petaled flowers on her skirt. Put tiny dots of green in the centers of the flowers.

Using a No. 2 green cone, make a yarn hat for the boy. Put a red No. 2 yarn around the middle of the hat, and tie the red yarn at the wrists.

With a No. 2 green cone, tie the yarn at the ankles and make a bow knot at the neck.

Make the branches of the small Christmas tree with a ⅛-inch V-cone of green icing. Decorate the tree with balls of red and gold icing.

Make faces on doll heads with brush and black or dark blue vegetable coloring.

Drop No. 2 Christmas red buttercream icing (to represent yarn) from tops of dolls heads to top back margin of cake. Make several loops at this point. Then drop e-l-e design with No. 2 red cone around top edge and draw e-l-e design around upper side of cake. Make roping on top edge between two e-l-e designs.

FIG. 37 (37C, p. 73)

Draw e-l-e design with white No. 2 cone around lower side of cake. Make No. 5 white rope at inside base border. Finish outside base border with No. 2 red roping.

For more help, please study evergreen trees, p. 18; roping, p. 29; bows, p. 45.

CHRISTMAS TREE BELL CAKE

This white-iced cake is 12 inches square and 1½ inches high. (Fig. 38, p. 90.)

Press a long wire into the icing after it is dry to form evenly spaced lines. Then form other lines at right angles to first ones. Turn cake so that diamond pattern is emphasized.

Make four different sizes of small sugar bells. Using a No. 3 cone of soft buttercream icing, make hammers inside bells. Keeping cone at a medium angle, bring icing from inside top to inside edge, and then lift tube slightly to form round ball. Stop pressure and then move tube to one side. (No point of icing will mar the smooth surface if the latter technique is used.)

Place smallest bell at top of tree; two very small bells in second row; one very small bell, one small, one very small in third row; three small bells in fourth row; one small, two large, one small in fifth row; five large in sixth row; and six large bells in seventh row.

Make a bow of buttercream ribbon with a No. 125 cone.

Form borders with No. 5 white beadwork.

Before cutting cake, give sugar bells as souvenirs to guests.

For additional help, please study ribbons, p. 45; beading, p. 29; sugar bells, *DC*, pp. 89ff.

HOLIDAY BOUQUET

The white-iced loaf cake is 12 inches long, 4½ inches wide, and 2½ inches high. (Fig. 39, p. 91.)

Use a No. 5 cone and soft white buttercream icing to rope corners and top and base borders.

Make a drawing of a vase on parchment paper. Cut out vase carefully so that paper that is left can be used as a stencil.

FIG. 38 (38C, p. 74)

FIG. 39 (39C, p. 74)

When icing on cake is no longer sticky, press paper vase against icing until slight depression is formed. Remove paper vase.

Place paper stencil above vase-shaped depression in icing. Pour medium-granulated, gold-colored sugar through opening in paper stencil until vase-shaped depression in icing is filled. Remove paper stencil.

Make stems with No. 3 cone of dark green buttercream icing.

Use very small paper cone of soft medium green buttercream icing for evergreen.

Combine two parts of *very soft* dark green buttercream icing with one part piping gel. Use the mixture in a ⅜-inch V-cone to form holly leaves. Form points along edges of leaves with small, moist brush.

Make holly berries with fine paper cone of red piping gel.

Leaving open spaces between them, add dots of red piping gel to corners and base border. Add smaller dots of green piping gel between red ones.

If you need help, please study roping, p. 29; holly, *BCF*, p. 52.

CHRISTMAS CANDLES AND RIBBONS

Cover with white icing an oval-shaped cake (10 by 7¼ inches) on an oval-shaped baseboard (12 by 9½ inches). (Fig. 40, p. 75.)

After icing is crusted slightly, press clean, plastic, mesh fruit bag (or similar material) against it to achieve special surface texture.

Make two large red candles (in sections) with No. 27 star tube and rope technique. Use No. 104 cone of green icing to form a ribbon that starts at the top of the first candle and spirals to the bottom of the second candle. Alternate sections of ribbon and candle so that ribbon actually swirls around candles. Starting at the top, add fine beads of plain piping gel to edges of ribbon.

Add black wick to top of each candle with a No. 1 cone. Make candle flames with ¼-inch V-cone yellow. Add to center of flames additional red-tinged, yellow, much smaller flames with ⅛-inch V-cone. Touch edges of flames lightly with red color and brush. Add very small marks of yellow around flames to indicate light.

Noel is repeated with No. 101 red ribbon script around base of cake. Make No. 3 green dots between words.

Tie No. 102 green bows on side of cake. Add drop of uncolored piping gel to center of each bow.

Form top border with alternating white 101s bows and green dots. Make outside base border with No. 3 white beadwork.

If you need help, please study roping and beading, p. 29; ribbons and bows, p. 45; V-cone leaves, *DC*, pp. 41ff.

HOLIDAY PRAYER

For this cake you will need two 6-inch round layers, approximately 1½ inches high. Cut one layer at the edge and join them as shown in Fig. 41, p. 76. Cover them with white icing.

After icing is crusted make latitude and longitude lines with pin.

Draw some rough maps on paper and cut them out. Place patterns on thickened, earth-brown buttercream decorating icing that has been rolled out to ⅛-inch thickness.

Cut around patterns and remove them. Take away excess icing. Soften cut edges of icing maps with a gentle pressure from the cushions of your fingers. Place icing maps on cake.

Make band of holly and holly berries around sides of cake. Use No. 2 cone for dark green stems and ¼-inch V-cone for medium green leaves. Form holly berries with No. 1 red piping gel.

Use No. 1 cone for gold-colored icing on top and base borders. Use same cone for lettering *PEACE*. Notice that the two *E*s become birds.

If you need further help, please study birds, p. 36; holly, *BCF*, p. 52.

VII

VALENTINES

SWEETNESS CAKE

Cover a small, 8-inch, heart-shaped cake with white icing. (Fig. 42, p. 77.)

Make pink morning glory with modified petunia technique. (See *BCF*, pp. 190ff.) Add small yellow stamens with No. 2 cone.

Make green stems with No. 2 cone, tendrils with No. 1 cone, and heart-shaped green leaves with ⅜-inch V-cone and No. 3 cone. (See *BCF*, p. 47.)

Figure pipe hummingbird with No. 3 yellow and No. 2 brown. Form wings with stiff yellow icing and ⅜-inch V-cone leaf technique. Overpipe wings with a soft yellow No. 1 cone.

Make 23 No. 27 pink pop-ups. Make No. 2 yellow stamens in centers.

Form top border with No. 2 alternating white beadwork.

Form base border with No. 5 white beadwork. Add pink pop-ups and alternate them with hearts made with No. 5 green cone.

Using No. 2 cone of *very soft* brown icing, add to top inscription *I CAN'T GET ENOUGH OF YOUR SWEETNESS.*

If you need more help, please study birds, p. 36; beading, p. 29; hearts, *DC*, pp. 83f.; star pop-ups, *BCF*, pp. 18ff.

VALENTINE BOUQUET

Set 10-inch layer cake on 12-inch baseboard. (Fig. 43, p. 78.) Ice top of cake white and sides of cake and baseboard light blue.

Against white top of cake figure pipe light blue hearts with No. 5 cone of *very soft* icing. (Points of hearts should be near edge of cake.)

Bead top border and inside base border with No. 5 light blue cone. Bead outside base border with No. 3 white cone.

Bend a piece of soft wire to form an S shape. Bend ends of wire upward to form handles. Press wire lightly into blue icing on side of cake at six equally-spaced intervals. Bend a second piece of wire to form a *reverse* S shape. Press it lightly to the right of each of the first six imprints.

Using the imprints in the icing as a guide, figure pipe swans with a No. 5 cone and *very soft* white icing. Form them in such a way that the necks, heads, and beaks suggest the shape of hearts. (If the reader prefers, he can decorate the top of the cake with a wreath, corsage, or spray of flowers.)

Thicken a small amount of buttercream decorating icing with powdered sugar until it is the consistency of putty and will handle easily.

Dust a surface lightly with cornstarch. Roll the thickened icing out to ⅛-inch thickness with a small rolling pin. Cut it into rectangular pieces and place them on a flat, absorbent paper towel surface to dry.

Cut a parchment triangle that is approximately 12 by 15 by 19 inches. Make a cone that is 3 inches in diameter at the top. Fasten the cone at the side with masking tape. Even the top of the cone by cutting straight across the top. Cut into the top edge of the cone about ½ inch deep at ¾-inch intervals around the circumference. Fold flaps outward.

Make a ½ inch hole in the center of a 6-inch cardboard cake circle. Cut a wood dowel stick that is ½ inch thick and about 5½ inches long. Place the dowel in the center of the cone and stuff the cone with wads of paper towel to keep dowel in place. Place top of dowel stick through hole in center of 6-inch cake circle. Fasten flaps of paper cone to underside of cardboard circle with masking tape. Cover cone and underside of cardboard with green icing.

Cover a second 6-inch cardboard circle with green icing.

Make up 10 sweetheart roses with a No. 103 rose-pink cone. Using a ¼-inch V-cone of soft medium green icing, arrange roses in formal leaf setting at center of second cardboard.

Form a variegated pink and white No. 125 wavy ribbon around edge of second circle. Form a white No. 125 wavy ribbon that overlaps white edge of first ribbon. Border top edge of white ribbon with plain piping gel beadwork from a very small opening of a small paper cone.

Make a circle of violet leaves with a medium green, ½-inch V-cone. Point tops of leaves to outside of circle.

Make violets with No. 102 tube and violet and blue variegated icing. Use No. 2 yellow cone for centers. (The ice-can method was used for these because it is faster.) Place violets against leaves. (Other flowers can be used, of course, in place of this arrangement.)

Put spots of icing on top of first cardboard. Place bottom of second cardboard with flower arrangement against top of first cardboard. Place bouquet on top of cake so that edge of cardboard digs into white icing slightly; in this way, the bouquet will not roll to one side.

Put second variegated pink and white No. 125 wavy ribbon around edges of both cardboards so that edges will not show.

Make a bow of light pink and white variegated No. 125 ribbon around cone. Border both edges of ribbon with beading of plain piping gel.

Using the same color of violet icing that was used for the violets, letter inscription on buttercream card and border it with No. 2 beadwork. Place card on cake top and against front edge of bouquet.

The bouquet can be kept as a souvenir long after the cake has been enjoyed.

If you need further help, please study beading, p. 29; ribbons, p. 45; swans, p. 43; hearts, *DC*, pp. 83f.; roses, *DC*, pp. 49ff.; leaves, *DC*, pp. 41ff.; violets, *BCF*, pp. 150ff.

VALENTINE INTERNATIONAL

Cover a heart-shaped layer cake with white icing. (Fig. 44, p. 78.)

Use different styles and various colors for the lettering. Put heart-shaped flowers with stems and leaves among the words.

Make alternating No. 4 white beadwork around the top border.

Cut away a few beads at ten equally-spaced intervals around the top.

Make No. 3 green stems and receptacles on the side of the cake in such a way that the receptacles will help support the ten No. 103 pink nail roses that are placed on the top edge of the cake.

Add ⅛-inch V-cone sepals and ¼-inch V-cone leaves to receptacles and stems.

Run a No. 46 (corrugated side up) brown ribbon around the base of cake and over the bottoms of stems.

If you need further help, please study *DC*: hearts, pp. 83f.; beadwork, p. 80; nail roses, pp. 49f.; leaves, pp. 41f.

VALENTINES IN THE SKY

With a French knife trim the top edge of a 10-inch layer cake so that it is rounded. (Fig. 45, p. 79.) Place the cake on a 12-inch base. Cover the cake and baseboard with very light blue icing. Finish the edge of the baseboard with No. 4 very light blue beadwork.

Make a paper pattern for parachute top that is 2½ inches by ⅞ inch. Spread some pink and some blue buttercream icing on a cookie sheet. Place sheet in freezer for five minutes. Use pattern and a paring knife to cut out five blue and five pink parachute tops. If icing becomes too soft, return it to freezer for a few minutes.

Place tops in random fashion on top and sides of cake. Make hearts which are below parachutes with a No. 5 cone of *very soft*, light brown icing.

Drop No. 1 black threads of icing from parachutes to hearts. Mark tops of parachutes with a sharp knife. Form No. 2 white roping along lower edges of parachutes.

Put pink roses under blue canopies and red roses under pink canopies. Use nail rose technique and No. 103 tube. Surround roses with light green leaves made with a ¼-inch V-cone.

On either side of each heart put a few forget-me-nots, larger at the top, smaller at the bottom, with leaves between. Forget-me-nots can be white with yellow centers.

Using black icing in a No. 2 cone, divide the message *I LOVE YOU* on three of the hearts. Using No. 3 white cone, pipe lovebirds on tops of the same parachutes. Use a ¼-inch V-cone of white icing for wings.

If you need more help with individual techniques, please study beading and roping, p. 29; birds, p. 36; hearts, DC, pp. 83ff.; nail roses, DC, pp. 49ff.; leaves, DC, pp. 41ff.; forget-me-nots, DC, pp. 27ff.

VALENTINE FAN

The use of gum-paste pieces will add delicacy and uniqueness to the valentine in Fig. 46, p. 99. If you do not have some small, triangular-shaped pieces of gum paste on hand, make a small batch of gum paste (pastillage). Use recipe on p. 62 or any standard recipe. (Add mint flavor. Children of all ages like to eat the little sticks of candy.)

FIG. 46 (46C, p. 79)

When the gum paste is aged properly, roll out a small piece so that it is very thin. Then cut it into small, narrow triangles (about 3 inches long), and let them dry over a curved surface for 8 or 12 hours. (If you do not wish to use gum paste, you can substitute rows of buttercream star work against the cake.)

Cut paper pattern 11 inches by 8 inches. Place it on top of layer cake and cut around pattern. (Do not allow baseboard to project beyond edge of cake.) Ice cake with light pink icing.

Put two circles of No. 125 green violet leaves at the left and right top corners of the cake. Put a circle of ¼-inch V-cone green rose leaves in the top center area.

Make No. 103 pink nail roses and place them in the center arrangement. Add more leaves as roses are placed.

Using metal surface and freezing technique, make up thirty violets with a No. 103 variegated cone of orchid-violet icing. Place them on the violet leaf arrangements.

Place seven gum paste triangular pieces near bottom of cake. Make buttercream stars with Nos. 13 and 27 on top of gum-paste pieces so that the stars become gradually larger as they go away from the bottom edge. (If you chose not to use gum paste, just make the stars against the cake instead.)

Using a No. 4 cone of *very soft* white buttercream icing, drop straight lines from top area to star work.

Using the same cone, make beadwork to cover the ends of the lines just above the star work. Use beadwork for top and base borders of cake.

Add another pink No. 104 nail rose and green leaves at the bottom point of the cake.

If you need further help, please study the following: beading, p. 29; nail roses, *DC*, pp. 49ff.; rose leaves, *DC*, pp. 41ff.; violets, *BCF*, pp. 150ff.; violet leaves, *BCF*, p. 49.

TO MY LOVE

Bake cakes in heart-shaped pans, or cut heart-shaped cakes out of layer or sheet cakes. (Fig. 47, p. 101.) Use a paper pattern that is 5 inches wide. Ice cakes with white icing.

Make nail roses with a No. 104 pink cone and trim them well at the base before placing them.

FIG. 47 (47C, p. 79)

Use soft dark green icing for No. 3 stems, receptacles, and No. 1 leaf stems. Use soft pastel green icing for ⅛-inch V-cone sepals, ¼-inch V-cone small leaves, and ⅜-inch V-cone large leaves.

Do lettering with a No. 2 dark pink cone. Use roping on capitals.

Make No. 13 wide, white shells at top borders, and No. 13 narrow, pastel pink shells at base borders.

Display cakes against grease-resistant, pink satin ribbon and bow.

If you need help, please study the following pages in *DC*: nail roses, pp. 49ff.; leaves, pp. 29, 41ff.; roping, p. 66; wide shells, pp. 72f.; narrow shells, p. 72.

HEARTS AND DAISIES

This design can be used for a valentine, an engagement announcement, or an anniversary. (Fig. 48, p. 103.)

Make hearts with sugar or cake. Trim top edge of 10-inch round cake with a French knife. Place cake on 12-inch baseboard and ice cake and baseboard white. Make white icing on baseboard thicker at base of cake and thinner at edge of baseboard.

Using a light green No. 125 cone, place base of tube at center of top beveled edge of cake, turn cake and make two strips of icing around top edge. Smooth the two strips together with water and finger or brush.

Press the base of the No. 125 light green cone against the base of the cake at intervals and make a wavy border as the cake is turned. Make No. 4 light green bead borders for ribbons at base and top borders.

Using a No. 3 dark pink cone, figure pipe pairs of hearts at regular intervals on side of cake.

Place light pink and dark pink icings in a No. 125 cone so that the ribbon for the hearts will resemble a double-faced satin ribbon. (This will be much more beautiful than either a plain or a variegated ribbon.)

Place sugar or cake hearts on cake top. Edge the one at the left with No. 2 dark pink; alternate beads. Put a No. 103 light pink frilly border around the other one. Put names or other appropriate inscriptions on hearts.

Make daisies on pieces of waxed paper. Use a No. 7 nail, No. 5 golden yellow center dipped into coarse, golden yellow granulated sugar, and 3/16-inch V-cone white buttercream icing. Place daisies in freezer for five minutes.

FIG. 48 (48C, p. 80)

Make irregular daisy leaves with medium green ⅜-inch V-cone. Remove frozen daisies from papers and place them on leaves.

For further instruction, please study beading, p. 29; ribbons, p. 45; hearts, *DC*, pp. 83f.; sugar molding, *DC*, pp. 89ff.; daisies, *BCF*, pp. 80ff.; daisy leaves, *BCF*, pp. 50, 52.

YOU ARE THE ONE ROSE

This is a 10-inch, heart-shaped cake, 3 inches in depth, iced white on a baseboard that is half an inch beyond the edge of the cake. (Fig. 49, p. 105.)

Bend soft wire to form a heart shape with a handle. When the cake icing is no longer sticky, press wire form lightly into side of cake to leave patterns for hearts. Using soft red icing in a No. 5 cone, form hearts by making long beads in a V pattern.

Fold a sheet of paper and cut a heart-shaped pattern. Place pattern on top of cake and press lightly at edges to leave imprint in icing. Remove paper.

Use a No. 134 cone of *very soft* black icing to form musical staff in shape of heart. Divide staff at intervals with very fine black lines drawn at right angles to staff.

Using same technique as for hearts on side of cake, form hearts of musical notes with very small paper cone of red piping gel. Add flags to notes with very small cone of soft black icing.

Using a No. 7 nail, make a large nail rose with rose-colored icing and No. 125 cone. Form green No. 3 stems and V-cone leaves of different sizes.

Make top border by circling cake with No. 46 soft white cone (smooth side up), first with tube in horizontal position, and then with tube in vertical position at the side. Add No. 5 soft white beadwork where edges of ribbons come together.

Using No. 46 soft white icing (corrugated side up), circle cake twice at the base border.

If you need further instruction, please study the following pages in *DC*: leaves, pp. 41ff.; nail roses, pp. 49ff.; hearts, pp. 83f.

FIG. 49 (49C, p. 80)

VIII

ST. PATRICK HAT CAKE

Bake a pound cake in a Boston bread pan measuring 4 inches in diameter at one end, 3 inches at the other end, and 5½ inches in height. (Fig. 50, p. 108.)

Cut a one-layer, oval-shaped cake (8 inches by 6 inches) from a round 8- or 9-inch layer cake.

Set the two cakes together with icing, and cover completely with a light green icing. (Do not allow a baseboard to project beyond the cake.)

Where the cakes join together make two widths of No. 125 black icing and smooth them together with a moist brush to form a ribbon around the hat crown.

Make a gold buckle with three layers from a No. 104 cone and smooth layers together. Then mound extra black icing in center of buckle.

Using a darker shade than the one on the cake, make light green fern with ⅛-inch V-cone and No. 2 cone.

Make shamrocks on ribbon and between ferns with medium green icing and No. 3 cone.

Use thickened brown buttercream icing for mushrooms. (You may use marzipan if you wish.) Mold stems and caps separately by hand, put them together, and place them on hat brim. Cut edges of mushrooms here and there.

Using dark green piping gel and a small paper cone, figure pipe shamrocks on hat crown and beads on top border of crown and hat brim.

On waxed paper figure pipe leprechaun with *very soft* white buttercream icing. Put fringe of white hair and whiskers on sides of face with a fine paper cone.

With brush and vegetable colors make face, hands, and tips of ears flesh color (peach).

FIG. 50 (50C, p. 80)

Color jacket, tie, hat, and socks green; shoes, brown; and put black dots in centers of green eyes.

Freeze leprechaun, remove from paper, and place him against right side of buckle.

If you need further help, study shamrocks, *DC*, pp. 83f.; figure piping heads, *DC*, pp. 86f.; ferns, *BCF*, pp. 69f.; mushrooms, *BCF*, p. 70.

IX

EASTER FANTASY

Cover 10-inch layer cake and 12-inch baseboard with white icing. (Fig. 51, p. 137.)

Make paper or cardboard pattern for basket, large leaves and tulip. Press pattern into crusted icing so that imprint remains when pattern is removed.

Fill tulip area with soft red buttercream icing. Smooth surface with moist brush or finger. Outline petals with No. 2 cone of golden brown icing.

Make large green stem and large green leaves in a similar way.

Fill in basket area with horizontal lines of pink No. 3 stretched roping. Form basket edge with golden brown No. 5 roping.

Make five petaled, fantasy flowers with gold No. 3 centers and No. 3 orchid or red petals. Put dots of red on the centers and dots of white on the petals.

Form green stems with No. 2 cone and green leaves with ¼-inch V-cone. Indicate veins on small leaves with golden brown No. 1 cone.

Outline two large leaves with No. 2 golden brown cone and form scroll pattern on leaves with same cone.

Figure pipe white rabbits with No. 5 white cone. Put pink icing in ears and on nose. Make a pink bow tie on rabbit at left side of basket. Dot eyes and outline rabbits with black vegetable color and a brush. Give rabbits black mustaches if you wish.

Figure pipe running rabbits around the side of the cake with a No. 3 cone of golden brown icing.

Bead the top border with a No. 3 cone of white icing, and bead the inside base border with a No. 5 cone. Alternate orchid and red thick No. 13 stars around the outside base border.

If you need further help, please study beading and roping, p. 29; rabbits, p. 39; fantasy flowers, DC, pp. 39ff.; leaves, DC, pp. 41ff.

X

MOTHER'S DAY

ORCHIDS FOR MOTHER

If you do not have some small, thin, narrow, curved ornamental pieces of gum paste on hand, make a small batch of gum paste (pastillage). Use recipe on p. 62 or any standard recipe.

When the gum paste is aged properly, roll out a small piece so that it is very thin. Then cut some of it into narrow strips (⅛ inch wide and 2½ inches long), and let them dry over a curved surface for 8 or 12 hours. Cut out some quarter-moons with a 2-inch cookie cutter and dry them on a flat surface.

Make paper pattern 8½ inches by 8½ inches. Put pattern on top of a cake that is 2 or 2½ inches thick. Cut around pattern. (Fig. 52, p. 114.)

Place pattern on some heavy cardboard. Mark and cut cardboard so that it will extend ½ inch beyond the cake when it is used as a baseboard. Ice cake and baseboard light green.

Make four buttercream orchids directly on the top of the cake with white icing and Nos. 5, 104, and 125 tubes and a ¼-inch V-cone. Make centers of orchid slippers with No. 3 yellow cone. Brush inside of slippers with yellow vegetable color.

Push four quarter-moon pieces of gum paste into the sides of the cake, near the top and inside the indented curves. Decorate the tops of pieces with small, five-petaled fantasy flowers. Use light pink No. 3 cone for petals, yellow No. 2 cone for centers, and green No. 2 cone for leaves.

Using same light green icing as for cake, pipe No. 13 shell work at inside and outside base borders.

Evenly space five thin, narrow, curved gum-paste pieces in each space between quarter-moon pieces. Place them upright so that the bottom of

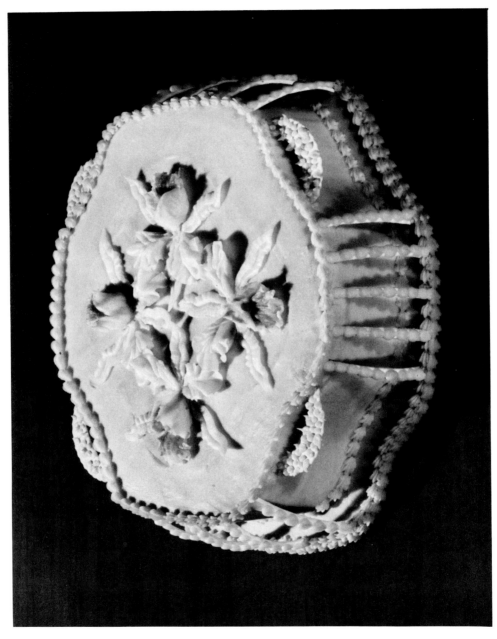

FIG. 52 (52C, p. 138)

each piece is braced outward against the base border, and so that the top of each piece is pushed into the icing just below the top edge of the cake. (Break off part of gum-paste piece if it is too long.)

Using a No. 4 cone of *very soft* white icing, put beadwork on upright pieces of gum paste.

Using same light green icing as for cake, pipe No. 13 shell work at top border. Pipe a second outside base border of No. 13 shell work to cover edge of cardboard base.

If you need further help with orchids, please study *BCF*, pp. 221f.

MOTHER'S DAY—EVERY DAY

Bake an angel food or pound cake in a 9-inch or 8-inch bowl, as for a doll cake. Add a baked, upside-down cupcake to the top of the baked, upside-down, bowl-shaped cake and seal together with icing. Cover the cupcake with an upside-down ice-cream cone (tall, cone-shaped variety). (Fig. 53, p. 138.)

Cover cake and cone with a light green icing. Place iced cake on a 10-inch baseboard that is iced chocolate.

Use the finest edge of an icing comb against the green icing on the bowl-shaped part of the cake so that the icing will resemble grass. Use comb against chocolate-iced base.

With a ½-inch V-cone of medium green icing, start at the base of the cone (the widest part) and form branches of evergreen tree. Part way up the tree, switch to a ⅜-inch V-cone and make smaller branches.

Form bird's nests on several branches with a No. 3 cone of butter-cream icing. Make birds with No. 2 cone of *very soft* white icing.

Create five-petaled fantasy flowers with No. 3 cones of red, orange, and orchid icing. Make yellow centers.

Figure pipe hen and two chicks at left with No. 5 white, No. 3 yellow, and No. 1 orange; duck and two ducklings with No. 5 white, No. 3 yellow, No. 2 red; rabbits and two baby bunnies with No. 3 and No. 2 white. Add dots of black icing for eyes.

This cake might be used for Mother's Day, Easter, a child's birthday, or just to celebrate that happy feeling we all get in the spring.

If you need help, please study birds, p. 36; rabbits, p. 39; fantasy flowers, *DC*, pp. 39ff.; leaves, *DC*, pp. 41ff.; chicks, *DC*, pp. 84f.

TABLECLOTH CAKE

Cover a 6-inch layer cake that is 4½ inches high with a thin layer of white icing. Place it on a baseboard that is 8 inches in diameter. (Fig. 54, p. 139.)

Thicken some buttercream decorating icing (see recipe on pp. 191-192) with sifted powdered sugar until it is the consistency of putty. Dust a board with cornstarch and roll out the thickened icing as you would pie crust.

Cut a circle of icing that is 3/16 inch thick and 8 inches in diameter. Place it on top of the cake so that it rounds over the top edge and down the side about one inch.

Roll out rectangular strips about 5 inches wide and 6 inches long. Hang them in folds from top circle. Seal them to top circle and to each other with light pressure of fingers, and make surfaces smooth by brushing lightly with the cushions of your fingers. Cut excess icing away from outer edge of baseboard.

Add border of No. 46 (plain side up) pink, regular buttercream decorating icing to bottom edge. Pipe continuous No. 2 beadwork at top and bottom edges of pink border.

Add to cloth simple fantasy flowers made with No. 2 pink and No. 1 green cones.

Make small dish of white, thickened buttercream decorating icing, and fill it with blue-green piping gel to represent water. Float green rose leaves (⅛-inch V-cone) and pink nail roses made with No. 101s cone. Place dish on table. If you wish, lean against the dish a thickened buttercream card with "Happy Mother's Day" or other message.

If you need more help, please study *DC:* beadwork, p. 80; fantasy flowers, pp. 26ff.; leaves, pp. 41ff.; nail roses, pp. 49ff.

XI

FATHER'S DAY CAKE

Cover with white icing a cake that is 11 inches by 4½ inches, and 2½ inches deep. When top surface is slightly crusted, roll grooved rolling pin over it lengthwise, or use coarse edge of icing comb. (Fig. 55, p. 140.)

On sides and ends use brush and vegetable colors. Indicate very light blue sky in upper part; green-blue water in lower part.

Make a paper pattern that is 10 inches long, 3¼ inches at the largest bottom width, and 2¼ inches wide at the top.

Use thickened, light lavender blue buttercream decorating icing for tie. After dusting a board with cornstarch, use a small rolling pin to roll out icing about ⅛ inch thick and 5 or 6 inches longer than the pattern, becoming narrower than the pattern at the top. Put pattern on top of the icing and cut around it except at the top. Remove pattern.

Lift up tie with long, wide spatula enough to fold very narrow top part under the main body of the tie, which is indicated by the pattern. Lift entire tie and place it on top of cake. Smooth out any wrinkles or imperfections in surface with cushions of finger tips until icing is as smooth as cloth.

Make simple sailboat pattern about 1⅝ inches wide and 2 inches high. Roll out more of same thickened icing until it is about 1/16 inch in thickness. Using sailboat pattern, cut out eight icing sailboats.

Place one of them at each end of the cake and three on each side. Add masts and spars with No. 2 brown cone.

Trace boat pattern on tie with pin. Fill in design with very fine No. 1 dots of brown and white icing to resemble embroidery. Make waves and gulls with No. 1 white.

Form top border and corners with No. 5 white rope. Make base C-scroll border with No. 5 aqua-green. Make whitecaps on C-scroll with No. 2 white.

Pipe gulls on sides and ends of cake with No. 2 brown.

For further help, please study DC: roping, pp. 66f.; C-scroll, p. 77.

117

XII

WEDDING CAKES

ALASKAN WEDDING CAKE

When our niece wanted me to give her away in marriage last summer, I readily agreed. When we found out that the marriage was to be in Alaska, we called the travel agent. When she wanted me to do the wedding cake, I pondered the distance between Michigan and the 49th State. (Fig. 56, p. 141.)

We agreed to do the decorating providing certain conditions were met. Since about 75 guests were expected, the family in Palmer, Alaska, were to provide a white-iced, 12-inch cake on a suitable baseboard, and a white-iced, 8-inch cake. They were also asked to provide an appropriate separator.

Since we were going to Alaska by plane, I packed decorating materials and equipment very carefully in our flight bag, which we kept with us at all times: colors, tubes, flower nail, icing, paper, gum-paste pieces, sugar bells, yellow sugar.

The bride wanted green and yellow as a color scheme and no conventional ornament on top.

To duplicate the cake you see here, please use the following directions: Cover up the flat circular surfaces of the separator as much as possible— white icing on top and light green icing on the bottom, with an alternating green No. 13 shell border. Then wind No. 2 green stems and ⅛-inch V-cone leaves around the pillars.

Place the 12-inch cake on the lacy baseboard, the separator on the 12-inch cake, and the 8-inch cake on top of the separator.

If you do not have some small, curved, 3-inch ornamental strips of gum paste (pastillage) and some 3-inch quarter-moon pieces of gum paste on hand, and do not know how to make them, please see p. 62 for recipe and p. 113 for make-up procedure.

Place eight narrow, curved strips of gum paste in wagon-wheel fashion on top of the cake. Make a large yellow nail rose with a No. 125 cone and place it at top center.

Make eight white daisies with a 3/16-inch V-cone and a No. 5 orange-yellow center. Press centers down into yellow, medium granulated sugar. Freeze daisies for five minutes, remove them from papers, and place them between gum-paste pieces.

Using a No. 27 white cone, make shell work out from center on tops of gum-paste pieces and around top edge of 8-inch cake. Add four ½-inch V-cone green leaves to base of rose.

Make four small white orchids between pillars and against green base of separator. Use Nos. 125, 104, and ⅜-inch V-cone for white petals. Add yellow to center of slippers with No. 3 cone and brush, using yellow vegetable color.

Add four sets of lovebirds to each tier with No. 3 cone of *very soft* buttercream white icing.

Put four sets of sugar bells at base of 12-inch tier. Using No. 13 yellow cone, add stars to rims of bells. Add yellow hammers to bells with No. 3 cone.

Place 12 quarter-moon gum-paste pieces around top edge of 12-inch tier. Make No. 27 white stars on top of quarter-moons. Make two tiers of No. 1 buttercream thread work hang from each quarter-moon and from top edge of separator. Form No. 3 white beadwork at top edge of separator.

Using No. 27 star tube, make four buttercream latticed effects at base of cake. (See p. 50.)

Using No. 5 cone of *very soft* white buttercream icing, make beadwork at base of 8-inch tier, at base of separator, and at top and base borders of 12-inch tier. Make bead tassels between each quarter-moon.

If you need further help, please study beading, p. 29; birds, p. 36; thread work (very small drapery), DC, p. 78; sugar bells, DC, pp. 89ff.; roses, DC, pp. 49ff.; daisies, BCF, pp. 80f.; small orchids, BCF, pp. 221f.

OHIO WEDDING CAKE

A year ago one of my nieces (my wife's namesake) in Delaware, Ohio, wanted her uncle to drive down from Detroit on Saturday, decorate her wedding cake, and attend the wedding and reception in the evening.

She arranged for Mrs. James Bailey to bake and ice the cake. Mrs. Bailey and Mrs. Lawrence Avey brought the cake, a turntable, and a separator to the church kitchen.

When I arrived they were there to help me in any way they could. This was fortunate because I didn't have too much time. (Fig. 57, p. 142.)

Not until I saw the cakes did I know what size they were. So I spent the first hour planning what the design would be. The bride had specified no bride-and-groom ornament. Her color scheme was lavender and blue, and she wanted some sugar bells and roses included in the decorations.

Before we left Detroit Mrs. Snyder made up a beautiful arrangement of bows, using lavender and blue satin and white lacelike gift-wrap ribbons. This was made so that it could be fastened securely to the cake and removed easily later on. I made the roses and sugar bells in advance.

For those readers who would like to try a similar design, proceed as follows:

Cakes are 14, 12, 10, and 8 inches in diameter. The separator is 10 inches.

Cover cakes and lower surface of separator with white icing. Use plastic or wooden supports in first, second and third tiers.

Make base border and inside borders between first and second tiers, and third and fourth tiers, with No. 30 white shell work.

Before putting the top two tiers on the separator, make four orchid-colored orchids (with yellow throats) on top of the second tier. Use tubes Nos. 104, 124, 5, and ¼-inch V-cone.

Mark off twelve equally spaced intervals around top edge of the first tier. Draw No. 3 light green stems in upside-down e-l-e design on side of first tier for formal wisteria design. Make bunches of wisteria with No. 103 lavender cone. Add tendrils with very fine paper cone of light green icing.

Space evenly No. 125 lavender nail roses at twelve places at base of cake, mismatching the wisteria above them. Add light green ½-inch V-cone leaves to roses.

Make a double row of No. 27 shells for outside top border of first tier. Make a single row of No. 27 shells for outside top borders of rest of tiers. Make a similar border for base of third tier.

Fasten ribbon ornament into top tier. Place four medium bells with white hammers so that they come out from under ribbons and rest on outside border. Place eight sets of small bells with white hammers on outside border of second tier.

Using a piece of bent soft wire for a pattern, press it into icing lightly at top side of top three tiers to form eight draperies. (Notice that wire must be bent differently for each tier.)

Make light blue forget-me-nots with tube No. 138 along impressions in icing left by wire. Form tassels also with forget-me-nots. (Press tube into the cake so that center post is below surface of icing, and then press out flower.) Add dot of yellow icing to center of each flower. Make tiny leaves (pressure technique) with No. 2 green cone between flowers.

If you need more help, please study *DC*: pressure technique leaves, p. 29; nail roses, pp. 49ff.; sugar bells, pp. 89ff. Study also *BCF*: orchids, pp. 221f.; wisteria, pp. 118ff.; forget-me-nots, pp. 145ff.

GOLDEN WEDDING ANNIVERSARY

Mr. and Mrs. Niles Graden of Dearborn, Michigan, who are the parents of our son-in-law, Mr. Ralph Graden, graciously gave permission for publication of this picture of their Golden Wedding Cake, which I was happy to decorate for them. (Fig. 58, p. 143.)

The tiers are 16, 12, 10, and 8 inches in diameter. The swan separators are 12 and 10 inches in diameter. The baseboard is decorated with gold nylon lacelon.

Cover all tiers and lower surfaces of separators with white icing. Comb icing on separator surfaces. Using a No. 104 cone of white icing, zigzag all inside and outside borders.

With a No. 5 cone of *very soft* white icing pipe sets of buttercream swans on the sides of the second and third tiers, directly below the swan pillars.

Place four sets of small sugar bells at equal intervals around the base of the ornament, which has been purchased previously. Put a small white rosebud, made with a No. 104 cone, between each set of bells. Pipe white hammers with a No. 3 cone in sugar bells. Add white leaves to the roses with a ¼-inch V-cone.

Make four corsages of buttercream gold-colored roses (deep yellow with touch of red and brown) on ledge between first and second tiers. Place them between pairs of swans. Make large rose in center of each corsage with a No. 125 cone; make medium roses and rosebuds with a No. 104 cone. Insert large, medium, and small gold artificial leaves around roses.

Place four medium sugar bells (with gold-colored hammers) in centers of the second and third tiers. Between pillars, near the edge, make white orchids with golden yellow throats. Use tubes Nos. 104, 125, 5, and ¼-inch V-cone.

Place triangular pieces of curved gum paste against side and base of top tier. Make white No. 27 buttercream shells on each gum-paste, ornamental piece. Make them small at the top and larger and larger as they approach the base.

Push both ends of eighth-moon, gum-paste, ornamental pieces into the side of the first tier. Make uniform No. 13 stars or shells on the outer edges of the pieces.

If you need further study, see the following: gum-paste, ornamental pieces, p. 62 and p. 100; swans, p. 43; nail roses, *DC*, pp. 49ff.; sugar bells, *DC*, pp. 89ff.; orchids, *BCF*, pp. 221f.

SECOND OHIO WEDDING CAKE

A second niece in Delaware, Ohio, wanted me to decorate her wedding cake. She wanted yellow to be the dominant color, with roses, orchids, daisies, and sugar bells included in the decoration. (Fig. 59, p. 144.)

Since this work was to be done on a weekend between classes in Detroit, I needed assistance. My niece persuaded Mrs. Lawrence Avey, who had helped me with the first Ohio Wedding Cake (June, 1974, *Mail Box News*), to help me again.

Mrs. Avey baked and iced beautifully cakes that were 14, 12, 10, and 8 inches in diameter. Plastic supports were used in the first, second, and third tiers. Her home became my workshop. Her daughter helped, and Mr. Avey transported the cake and took the picture of the finished wedding cake. The project was a very pleasant and successful experience because of their cooperation.

I brought from Detroit narrow, curved, gum-paste strips (see recipe on p. 62), small sugar bells, yellow sugar, thirteen large yellow buttercream roses, sixteen small yellow rosebuds, sixteen large white daisies with yellow centers, sixteen small daisies, forty-eight No. 13 yellow star pop-ups with green centers, and buttercream and royal icing.

If you wish to duplicate the cake in the photograph, proceed as follows:

Ice base of separator with white icing. Using same icing that was used on cake, make first tier base border with No. 30 shells. Make No. 27 shell work at rest of inside and outside borders.

Place sixteen narrow, curved gum-paste pieces on the top tier like spokes of a wheel. Cover them with No. 13 white shell work. Place a large, No. 125 yellow rose at the center of the wheel. Add four large ½-inch V-cone green leaves to rose. Put a small rosebud (No. 104) on each of the spokes and add ⅛-inch V-cone leaves to roses.

Place sixteen ⅛-inch V-cone small daisies around ledge where third and fourth tiers join. Place sixteen ¼-inch V-cone large daisies around ledge where first and second tiers join. Make daisy leaves between flowers with a green ¼-inch V-cone.

Place twelve large (No. 125) yellow roses around base of cake. Add ½-inch V-cone green leaves.

Make buttercream string drapery net against side of top tier with No. 2 cone, and against side of second tier with No. 3 cone.

Form shell drapery with shell tassels on side on third tier with No. 27 cone, and on side of first tier with No. 30 cone.

Make lavender orchids on white-iced separator base with Nos. 104, 125, and 5 cones, and ¼-inch V-cone. Add No. 3 yellow to centers and paint inside of slippers with very soft yellow icing.

Wind posts with No. 2 green stems. Add small ⅛-inch V-cone leaves. Attach No. 13 yellow star pop-ups (with green centers) to stems.

Put a little soft icing on the bottom edge of each small sugar bell. Press bottom edge lightly into yellow sugar and lift it away. Add yellow hammer with No. 3 cone and bulb technique. Place sixteen sugar bells by twos on either side of four posts.

Using royal icing in a very fine paper cone, make two tiers of thread work veiling (similar to drapery net against sides of second and fourth tiers) that hang from the bottom edge of the third tier.

If you need further instruction, please study *DC*: sugar bells, pp. 89ff.; roses, pp. 49ff.; rose leaves, pp. 41ff.; shells, pp. 72ff.; shell drapery, p. 79; string drapery, p. 78; royal-icing recipe, p. 124. Study also *BCF*: daisies, pp. 80f.; daisy leaves, pp. 52f.; star pop-ups, pp. 13ff.; orchids, pp. 221f.

XIII

DOUGHNUTS FOR THE BRIDE AND GROOM

DOUGHNUTS FOR THE BRIDE

There is a legend that the first doughnut was used for a wedding ring. As a consequence, doughnuts are a natural for wedding showers, breakfasts, and informal receptions. Fancied up a bit, they are not only extra delicious, but they are also likely to steal the show. (Fig. 60, p. 145.)

Make or buy some cake doughnuts—small ones for the bride, larger ones for the groom. Carve out the holes in the centers if they are not large enough. Trim some of them so that they are flat on one edge and then stand them upright. Stuff the trimmings into the centers of other doughnuts so they will be flat on top. Cut others in half and stand the halves upright.

To form the double wedding ring shown here, cut halfway through a doughnut along one-quarter of its circumference. Remove the cut portion. Place the edge of a second doughnut into the cavity of the first one. Mark the second doughnut with a knife and remove the cut portion. Place the two doughnuts together.

Mix together 5 pounds of confectioner's sugar, 5 pounds of fondant, 1¼ pints of hot water, a pinch of salt, and some vanilla, butter, or other flavor. The amount of water is variable because of differences in materials and weather conditions. For satisfactory results this icing has to be considerably thicker than that which would be used for petit fours because of the rougher and darker surfaces to be covered.

Put a screen on a baker's sheet. Rub excess crumbs off some of the trimmed and shaped doughnuts and place them on the screen. Have the smooth sides up.

Pour the white icing over one of them. If the glaze is too thin, add more powdered sugar to the icing. If the glaze is too thick, add a little water. When the icing is the right consistency, pour it over the other doughnuts, making sure that all the edges are glazed properly.

Fix a second baker's sheet and screen with doughnuts and pour delicate pastel shades of icing over them. Keep excess icing in a tightly covered container. It does not require refrigeration.

After the glaze has set, carefully lift doughnuts from screens with a spatula and place them on clean baker's sheets. Avoid damaging the glaze with your fingers.

Use light blue or pink buttercream icing with a No. 138 tube (forget-me-not tube) to make flowers on upright, white-glazed doughnuts. Hold tube at a right angle to the surface, push metal center shaft below glazed surface, and use light pressure on the buttercream icing. Put light yellow dots in centers of flowers. Using a No. 2 cone of pastel green icing and leaf-pressure technique, insert dainty leaves between the forget-me-nots.

Form pink birds on double-ring doughnut with No. 2 tube and figure-piping technique. Make rings and ribbons with No. 1 pink cone. Pipe beaded borders with same cone.

Using No. 102 light pink cone, make nail roses for filled-in doughnuts. Add light green rose leaves with ¼-inch V-cone. Make borders with No. 2 light pink cone and alternating bead technique.

Make pink orchid with No. 102 cone and ¼-inch V-cone. Insert small yellow center in slipper. Use white No. 2 cone for alternating bead border.

Make white lilies of the valley against light blue glazed doughnuts. Use No. 1 tube for stems and No. 2 tube for flowers.

If you need further help, see notes at the conclusion of "Doughnuts for the Groom," p. 128.

DOUGHNUTS FOR THE GROOM

Remember to use larger doughnuts for the stag party, wedding breakfast, or informal wedding reception. (Fig. 60, p. 145.)

The doughnuts for the bride were iced white and various pastel colors. Take the excess icing from the baker's sheets, add melted chocolate to it, and pour it over the large doughnuts.

The chocolate-glazed doughnuts are decorated similarly. Use white for forget-me-nots, light yellow for centers, and light green for leaves. Use birds, rings, and bead borders on double-ring doughnut.

FIG. 61 (61C, p. 145)

Cover chocolate glaze center of daisies with dots of yellow. Use ¼-inch V-cone of white icing and leaf technique for petals.

Make white nail roses with No. 104 cone. Make light green rose leaves with ⅜-inch V-cone. Use No. 2 white cone for alternate bead border.

Use No. 3 white cone and figure-piping technique for wedding bells and hearts.

Many other combinations of colors and designs will suggest themselves as you work; the possibilities are endless.

If you need more help, please study: beading, p. 29; birds, p. 36; figure-piped bells, p. 52; roses, DC, pp. 49ff.; leaves, DC, pp. 41ff.; lilies of the valley, DC, pp. 43ff.; hearts, DC, pp. 83f.; orchids, BCF, pp. 221ff.; daisies, BCF, pp. 80f.

XIV

FIRECRACKER CAKE

The white-iced cake is 13 inches by 9½ inches by 1¾ inches (Fig. 61, p. 127.)

Use a No. 2 cone of light gray icing for the fuses.

Use a No. 5 cone of *very soft* orange-red icing for firecrackers. Hold the tube in a horizontal position and off the surface of the cake. Fasten the icing to the fuse and bring it away from the fuse to form a firecracker. Finish both ends of firecrackers with circles of No. 2 orange-red icing.

Sprinkle a little coarse, yellow-orange granulated sugar to simulate sparks when fuse is lighted.

Spread a thin layer of very light gray icing on waxed paper. Put the icing in the freezer to harden, and remove it from the freezer after three or four minutes. Then place an open matchbox on top of frozen icing and cut away the excess. Refreeze icing, place it face down against the cake, and peel off paper. With a knife mark places where matchbox would bend.

Holding cone straight down and pressing tube into icing slightly to flatten it as it comes out of tube, figure pipe light gray matches with a No. 3 tube. Add green beads to matches.

Freeze another very light gray strip of icing and place it over bottoms of matches. Make black sandpaper strip with No. 46 (smooth side up) black cone. Make burnt match with No. 3 light gray cone and No. 2 black cone.

Make scroll roping at base by alternating No. 27 cones of red, white, and blue. Form an upside-down U that is large at the left and small at the right. Insert tube in hollow portion of first upside-down U when making second upside-down U, etc.

Move white No. 27 cone back and forth to form top border. Use same cone to form tassels at four corners.

For a little extra excitement when the cake is being cut, have someone light a string of firecrackers just outside a nearby window.

For a quieter bit of excitement, stand sparklers upright in the cake and light them before the cake is served.

For lots of excitement, light sparklers and firecrackers at the same time!

XV

BON VOYAGE

BON VOYAGE!

Place a 10-inch octagonal cake (3¾ inches high) on a 12-inch baseboard. Ice top white; ice sides light blue. (Fig. 62, p. 146.)

Using thin paper, trace a very old map of the world. Transfer the outline of the continents, etc., by placing thin paper on top of cake and punching small pin holes along lines on paper. Lift paper pattern away from cake.

Using No. 2 cones of icing and following pin marks in white icing, outline Europe and the Americas in red; Africa, Unknown Territory (below South America) and Australle (Incognve, unknown) in yellow; and Asia in green. Using a No. 2 cone, make a couple of black monsters cavort in what we now call the South Atlantic Ocean.

Print:

NOVA TOTIUS

TERRARUM ORBIS

GEOGRAPHICA 1670

with black No. 1 cone. With same cone print names of oceans and continents.

In the side panel at the left use light brown icing on the base to represent desert land. Make saguaro cactus with No. 30 and No. 27 yellow-green cones. Make barrel cactus with No. 30 green cone. Add white dots with yellow centers to tops of saguaro arms to indicate flowers. Add dots of red to top of barrel cactus to indicate flowers. Put a round, yellow sun in the sky.

In the center panel use green icing on the base and comb it to represent a grassy slope. Figure pipe a ming tree with a No. 3 cone of soft dark brown icing. Make leaves with No. 1 light yellow-green cone. Brush very soft white icing in sky to represent clouds. Make birds with No. 1 brown cone.

In the right panel make ocean beach with light brown icing, and add granulated sugar to give the effect of sparkling sand. Make waves with No. 3 light blue-green and white cones. Form trunk of palm tree with No. 5 cone of green icing tinged with brown. Make palm branches with dark yellow-green ¼-inch V-cone and No. 1 cone of same icing. Make seagulls with No. 2 white cone. Touch bodies with a bit of brown.

Use other scenes in rest of panels: pine tree, maple tree, other cactus, etc. If you wish, repeat some of the scenes.

Make separators between panels with two layers of No. 27 light blue shells formed in columns.

Use white No. 27 rope at top border. Use No. 13 green rope for outside base border where grass is used in panel; use No. 13 brown rope in outside base border where sand or desert is portrayed in panels.

If you need more help, please study *BCF*: cactus, pp. 66f.; palm tree, pp. 66ff. The ming tree is making its debut in icing.

HAVE A GOOD TRIP!

Cover top of 10-inch round cake with light blue icing. Cover sides and 12-inch base with combed medium green icing. (Fig. 63, p. 147.)

Make road with light tan icing and smooth with moist brush. Add combed medium green icing to left side of the road. Make weeds on both sides of the road with dark green icing and a small paper cone.

Make flowers on both sides of the road and on the grassy slopes. Use No. 3 red cone for petals of larger flowers and No. 2 yellow cone for centers. Make petals for small flowers with No. 27 yellow cone and use No. 1 green cone for centers. Vary sizes of flowers to indicate distances.

Cut out picture of old-fashioned car and press the edges lightly into the icing to leave an imprint. Lift away pattern. Fill in imprint of body of car with very soft red icing in a No. 5 cone. Smooth icing with damp brush or finger.

Make steering wheel and wheel spokes with No. 2 black cone. Make upholstery, tires, fenders, and headlight with No. 5 black cone.

To make signs, freeze white icing on a small sheet of waxed paper. Cut frozen rectangular pieces with a paring knife and place them on cake to the left side of the road. Make posts for signs with No. 2 black cone.

Using No. 2 black cone, write at top of cake *Have a good trip—with lots of gas!*

Using a No. 1 black cone, on the larger sign print the following advertisement:

PLENTY of GAS
FILLERUP

On the other sign print:

48 Miles
AHEAD

Outline signs with No. 2 black cone.

TO THE FOUR CORNERS OF THE EARTH

Cover a one-layer, 9-inch square cake with white icing. (Fig. 64, p. 147.)

Using a No. 1 cone of black icing, print *To The FOUR CORNERS Of The EARTH* in the center. At each side, midway between corners, write *Bon Voyage*.

In the upper left corner make the trunk of a pine tree with a No. 5 cone of brown icing. Form the branches near the top with a ⅛-inch V-cone of dark green icing. Form the larger, lower branches with a ¼-inch V-cone. Add a touch of brown icing in several places to represent pine cones.

In the upper right corner make the trunk and branches of a maple tree with a No. 5 cone of brown icing. Using a No. 13 star tube of medium green icing, cover the branches with leaves. Leave parts of the brown branches visible.

In the lower left corner make the trunk of the saguaro cactus with a No. 30 star cone of yellow-green icing that is held in a position horizontal to the cake. Bring out branches made with a No. 27 cone. Make a barrel cactus with a No. 30 cone held horizontally. Add needles to both the barrel and saguaro cacti with a very small paper cone of light green icing. Add touches of color to represent flowers.

In the lower right corner make the trunk of a coconut palm with a No. 5 cone of medium green icing. Using a ¼-inch V-cone of yellow-green icing, make several leaflike branches at the top. Conceal these with fronds made with a No. 2 cone of light green icing. Drop a No. 2 line down the center of each branch. Add some brown coconuts with a No. 5 cone.

Make a C-scroll border around the top edge with a No. 16 white cone. Form a base border with No. 4 brown beadwork.

If you need further help, please study *BCF*, pp. 65ff.

XVI

HALLOWEEN

ON YOUR WAY! OLD GIRL!

Cover top of 10-inch round cake with light blue icing. (Fig. 65, p. 148.) Ice sides and 12-inch base with chocolate icing. Cover lower fourth of cake top with green icing and comb it to represent grass.

Using very light, liquid, brown vegetable color, brush some 2- and 3-inch vertical curved lines against the blue sky to represent some dried grasses and weeds. Brush some light brown color horizontally against the green grass.

Make white stars in the sky with a No. 13 cone, using a variety of pressures. The moon is orange-yellow. Freeze a thin layer of icing on waxed paper. When it is frozen cut out round shape and place it in the sky. Add features to face with No. 1 black cone. With the same cone make a few bats in the sky.

Make two main stems for sunflowers with No. 3 green cone. Make sunflower centers about ⅝ inch in diameter on squares of absorbent paper. Use chocolate icing base with No. 2 chocolate beading to represent seeds, or use chocolate candy shot or nonpareils to represent seeds.

Using a 3/16-inch V-cone, make two mismatching layers of orange-yellow petals so that each flower is about 1¼ inches in diameter. Dry flowers overnight and then freeze them just before removing them from the absorbent papers with a thin, sharp knife. (You may also freeze them for five minutes and use them immediately if you are in a hurry, but they will not hold their shape as well.)

Using same icing as for petals, make faces on flowers with a No. 2 cone. Put black dots in eyes.

Add ⅜-inch, V-cone green leaves to the stems before and after placing flowers. Lean the witch's broom against the left sunflower stem. Make handle with No. 2 chocolate cone; use No. 1 cone for orange-yellow straw.

Figure pipe a sleeping witch between the two stalks of sunflowers. Use *very soft* orange-yellow icing and No. 5 cone for face, No. 1 white cone for hair, No. 5 black cone for cloak, and No. 3 black cone for hat that rests on her stomach.

Make a small black cat at her feet and some larger cats, spaced around the sides of the cake, with a No. 3 black cone.

Using a No. 3 yellow cone, print in large capital letters on the baseboard:

ON YOUR WAY! OLD GIRL!

Make top and outside base borders with No. 5 chocolate beadwork.

If you need further help, please study: cats, p. 40; beading, p. 29; witch heads and hats, DC, pp. 86f.; sunflowers, BCF, pp. 78f.

TRICK OR TREAT?

Ice a square or rectangular cake with a very-light-colored chocolate icing. Ice the baseboard and make a No. 5 rope inside base border with the same icing. Use the same No. 5 cone for plain border line at top edge. (Fig. 66, p. 157.)

Construct porch with vertical No. 3 lines of dark chocolate icing; make steps and sidewalk with horizontal lines.

Pumpkin is yellow-orange; stem is dark brown. Front of pumpkin is irregular to indicate that it has a lighted jack-o'-lantern face.

Cat is black or dark brown with yellow eyes.

The little, would-be trickster is dressed in a white sheet. His tall, dark brown hat is decorated with yellow and is fastened under his chin with a brown strap. The handle of the striped, brown and yellow shopping

FIG. 51 (text, p. 111)

FIG. 52 (text, p. 113)

FIG. 53 (text, p. 115)

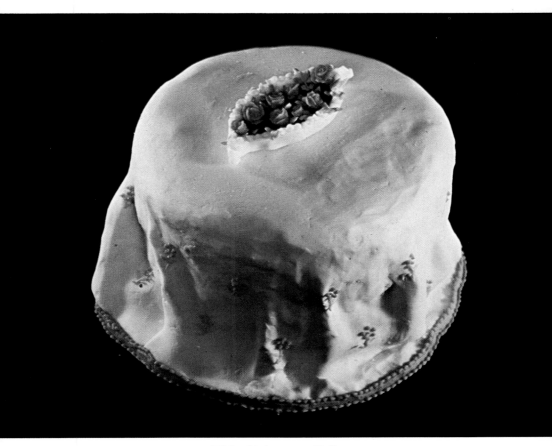

FIG. 54 (text, p. 116)

FIG. 55 (text, p. 117)

FIG. 56 (text, p. 119)

FIG. 57 (text, p. 121)

FIG. 58 (text, p. 122)

FIG. 59 (text, p. 123)

FIG. 60 (text, p. 125)

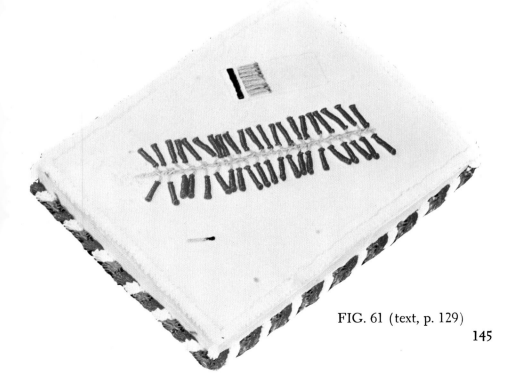

FIG. 61 (text, p. 129)

FIG. 62 (text, p. 131)

FIG. 63 (text, p. 132)

FIG. 64 (text, p. 133)

FIG. 65 (text, p. 135)

FIG. 66 (text, p. 136)

FIG. 67 (text, p. 159)

149

FIG. 68 (text, p. 161)

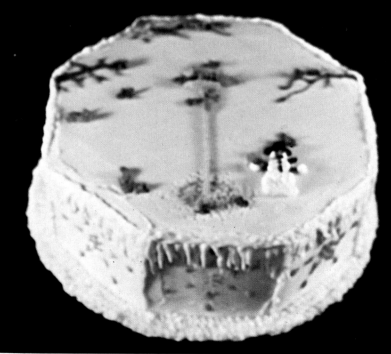

FIG. 69 (text, p. 162)

FIG. 70 (text, p. 162)

FIG. 71 (text, p. 165)

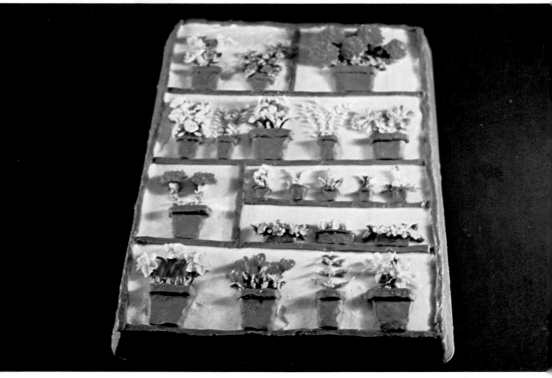

FIG. 72 (text, p. 166)

FIG. 73 (text, p. 166)

FIG. 74 (text, p. 167)

FIG. 75 (text, p. 168)

FIG. 76 (text, p. 168)

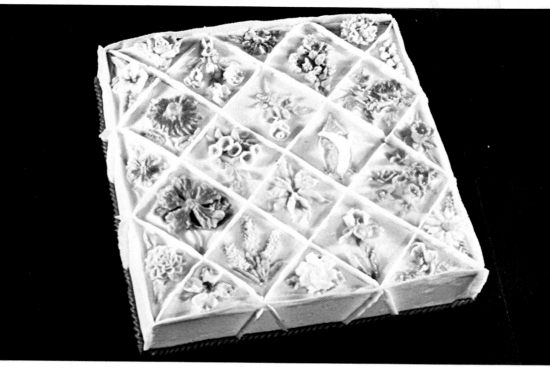

FIG. 77 (text, p. 169)

FIG. 78 (text, p. 170)

FIG. 79 (text, p. 172)

FIG. 80 (text, p. 174)

FIG. 66 (66C, p. 149)

bag is looped over his arm. His dark brown shoes protrude beneath the white sheet he is wearing.

The moon and stars are yellow. The tree branches, owl, and bats are dark brown.

The message is printed in white icing.

If you need more help, please study cats, p. 40; roping, p. 29; pumpkin, DC, pp. 86f.

XVII
THANKSGIVING

THANKSGIVING CENTERPIECE

Place a 10-inch square cake or dummy cake on top of a 14-inch square baseboard. (Fig. 67, p. 160.) Cover with white icing. Use large No. 5 white beadwork for inside base border.

Using *very soft* golden yellow icing and a No. 5 cone, make bunches of grapes along the baseboard.

Add medium green, five-part, divided grape leaves with ¼-inch V-cone. Smooth parts of each leaf together with moist brush and then add lines with pin. Make light green tendrils with *very fine* paper cone.

At the top of the cake sketch four cornucopias, each of which is 4½ inches in length. Then form the horns of plenty with golden yellow icing, No. 30 cone, and rope technique.

Make and freeze a variety of buttercream flowers: bronze mums, maroon and bronze gaillardias, scarlet hibiscus and oriental poppies.

Make a variety of green leaves suitable for the flowers you choose to make. Take frozen flowers out of freezer and place them on leaves in the arrangement. Add more leaves as necessary.

Finish top border with alternating small No. 5 white beadwork. Finish corners and outside base border with large No. 5 white beadwork.

If you need more help, please study beading, p. 29; grapes, p. 32; cornucopias, p. 31; grape leaves (similar to method for chrysanthemum leaves), *BCF*, pp. 49; flowers, *BCF*, see index.

FIG. 67 (67C, p. 149)

XVIII

FALL AND WINTER SCENES

FALL SCENE

Cover a 10-inch layer cake and 12-inch baseboard with white icing. (Fig. 68, p. 150.)

Using a pin, sketch lines into the icing where brown lines occur in the illustration.

Spread patches of thin light blue icing above top line. Add patches of thin white icing to same area. Blend the blue and white icing here and there with a small spatula to give a "clouds-in-the-sky" effect.

Put medium blue icing in pond area and give "small-waves" effect with a small spatula.

Cover rest of cake and baseboard with light green icing. Comb it with fine edge of decorating comb in many different directions to represent grass. (The white icing under the thin layer of light green icing will reduce the impact of the green and make the grass appear more as it does in late fall.)

Using medium brown soft icing and a small No. 3 cone, draw the brown lines marking the horizon, hills, and pond. With the same cone figure pipe the bird, dog, and the tree. Make a few dark shrubs at the right end of the pond.

With a small No. 3 cone of soft tan-colored icing, make brush, weeds, and rushes at various locations. Figure pipe a pheasant with the same cone. Add touches of black vegetable color with a brush to dog and bird.

If you need more help, please study birds, p. 36; dog (similar to rabbits in technique), p. 39.

WINTER STORY

Cover a 10-inch octagonal cake (4 inches high) and its 12-inch round baseboard with white icing. (Fig. 69, p. 150.)

Make bird feeder with No. 4 cone of green icing. Use two vertical, very fine black lines of icing to indicate sides of plastic seed container.

Make a pile of little dots of brown icing to represent seeds in the feeder. Make some brown seeds on the snow below the feeder and then press little marks into the snow to indicate bird and squirrel footprints.

Make a snowman with balls of white icing. Use No. 3 cone of black icing for a black hat and charcoal features and buttons. Make his arms with a stick of brown icing. Use large snowballs for his hands.

Using a gray-brown icing and a plain paper cone opening, make tree branches. Figure pipe squirrels with a No. 3 cone of golden brown icing. Make noses and eyes with a brush and black vegetable color. (Notice the squirrel on the ground who will eat the seed that's handy. The one on the pole is trying to get a paw on the feeder tray. The one on the tree branch above the feeder has another strategy in mind.)

Figure pipe brown sparrows, redbirds, and bluebirds with a No. 3 cone. Use a 1/8-inch V-cone for wings.

Press a plastic snowflake ornament against sides of cake in different positions to give patterns in the white icing. Use pink, blue, and lavender icing in a No. 2 cone to fill indentations. (Packaged decorations, including snowflakes, may be found at department store gift-wrapping counters.)

Use a No. 4 paper cone opening and white icing for irregular icicle design at the top border. Notice that icicles reach to base of cake at each of the eight corners.

Use No. 30 white, thick stars of irregular size to form base border.

If you need further instructions, please study birds, p. 36; squirrels (similar to rabbits in technique), p. 39.

WINTER SCENE

Place a two-layer rectangular cake, 13 inches by 9 inches, on a baseboard that extends one inch beyond the front of the cake. (Fig. 70, p. 151.) Cover the cake and baseboard with white icing. Ice lower two-thirds of top, front side, and projecting baseboard in a rough fashion to represent snowdrifts.

Brush light gray vegetable color about one-third of the way down from the back top border to achieve effect of horizon and vegetation in distance.

Use No. 1 light brown cone of icing for barn and snow fence. Use No. 1 dark brown cone of icing for trees, fence posts, and birds in flight.

Make Christmas roses with a No. 104 cone of white icing variegated with a touch of dark pink icing for the edges of the petals. Use No. 3 green and No. 2 yellow for centers. (If you need help, please study *BCF*, pp. 182ff. Christmas roses will blossom even when snow is on the ground.)

For leaves and stems use dark green icing, with brown icing laced through it with a table knife.

Make stems and green buds with No. 3 cone. Form leaves with ¼-inch V-cone. Make white buds with No. 3 cone.

Place Christmas roses on front baseboard and up against front side of cake.

Outline top borders at the back and the sides with brown No. 46 cone (smooth side up). Outline all base borders and the corners with the same cone.

XIX
FLOWER ARRANGEMENTS

NASTURTIUM CENTERPIECE

Bevel the edge of a thin 6-inch layer and place it on the top of a 10-inch round layer cake. Place both on a 12-inch baseboard. (Fig. 71, p. 151.)

Ice top and side white and baseboard brown. Comb brown icing in different directions. When top surface is crusted slightly, press plastic, mesh fruit bag (or similar material) against it to achieve special texture.

Form No. 3 green stems for flowers and leaves so that they start from the brown baseboard.

Make full nasturtiums for the top and half-nasturtiums on the side. Use yellow, orange, red, and mahogany-brown flowers.

Make three shades of green for leaves. Use flower nail, waxed paper, and freezing method, with No. 7 nail and No. 125 cones. Before placing flowers, put leaves on top, side, and base of cake.

Try this variation for half-nasturtiums. Instead of using the direct method, work with ice cans, or a metal surface and a freezer. Make petals for flowers and freeze them for five minutes.

Remove them with thin, small spatula and place each one over a No. 5 ball of icing against side of cake. Put down five petals for each flower in this manner. Extend each petal to center of flower with No. 5 cone of soft icing, using same color as flower.

Brush appropriate liquid vegetable colors on the inside of flower petals. After petals thaw, bend outer edges against cake and hide the balls of icing over which the petals are rounded.

Half-nasturtiums made in this way will appear three-dimensional when supported at the base and side of the cake.

If you need more help, please study *BCF*: full nasturtiums, pp. 192ff.; half-nasturtiums, pp. 194ff.; nasturtium leaves, p. 49.

WINDOW GREENHOUSE

Ice top of 10 inch-by-15-inch sheet cake with white icing. Ice sides with chocolate icing. (Fig. 72, p. 152.)

Make shelving and dividers with No. 46 (smooth side up) cone of dark chocolate icing.

Roll out orange-brown, thickened buttercream decorating icing to 3/8-inch thickness. Cut out different shapes and sizes for flowerpots. Cut strips and add to tops. Put pots on shelves.

Put a variety of flowers and greenery in the pots. You may use any you choose, but if you are following the illustration:

Top shelf: Petunias (No. 101 tube); holly (3/16-inch V-cone);
    peonies (No. 101), 3/16-inch V-cone leaves.
Third shelf: Bluebells (No. 13), 3/16-inch V-cone; fern, No. 1
    dark green stem, 1/8-inch V-cone, medium green leaves;
    iris (No. 101), 3/16-inch V-cone; fern; half-nasturtium (leaves, No.
    103; flowers, No. 101).
Second shelf: Carnations (No. 101), No. 5 light green, No. 2 dark green.
    Upper shelf: Ageratum; butterfly bush; hyacinth; snowdrop, monks-
        hood (101s).
    Lower shelf: Violets (No. 101s); cactus, No. 13; violets (No. 101s).
Bottom shelf: Daffodils (No. 101); half-tulips (No. 101); coleus; day lilies
    (3/16-inch V-cone for flowers, 1/8-inch V-cone for leaves).

If you need further help, please consult the index in *BCF* and study necessary text and illustrations.

FALL FLOWERS

Cover top of 10-inch square cake with white icing. (Fig. 73, p. 152.) Ice sides and one corner of top with chocolate icing. The latter, which will represent a planter's box, should be pointed toward the decorator as he arranges the flowers.

Border the top edge of the planter, as well as the top and the bottom edges, and the corners of the cake with *very soft* chocolate icing and No. 5 beadwork.

Make eleven or more gaillardia flowers, using No. 102 yellow cone for the petals and No. 5 chocolate cone for the centers. Dip the centers in yellow medium-granulated sugar. Using small brushes, paint liquid medium-brown vegetable color at the center and light scarlet red in the middle of the petals. (If you need further help with flower technique, please study *BCF*, p. 154.)

Make long No. 3 green stems for salvia and shorter stems for gaillardia. Put ¼-inch, V-cone, back-away, irregular, tapered leaves on the gaillardia stems, and ½-inch, V-cone, large, broad, tapered leaves on salvia stems.

Using No. 102 cone of scarlet red icing, make salvia flowers with two extended-center petals, at different angles and tilts, as for sweet-pea buds. Make flowers not only to the left and right of stems, but also out from center of stems. (Salvia are making their debut in buttercream in this book. We hope you like them.)

FLOWER TREE

The Flower Tree can be made as a cake dummy and used only as a centerpiece for many different occasions. (Fig. 74, p. 153.)

It can also be made of real cake, much as a doll cake is made. The upper part can be formed with an upside-down parchment cone. When it comes time to serve a real cake, the flowers can be removed and placed in small boxes for guests to take home as souvenirs. The top part can be saved for the honored guest, and the rest of the cake can be served.

Any variety of flowers may be used. If you choose the variety in the illustration, make up in advance: nail roses, *DC*, pp. 49ff.; from *BCF*, daffodils, pp. 165ff.; tulips, pp. 203ff.; gardenias, pp. 24ff.; daisies, pp. 80f.; violets, pp. 150ff.

Cover the whole tree with a very light green icing. Place flowers in a scatter design. To make sure the large ones will not fall off, make hollow places in the icing first, then place the flowers, and then make leaves in strategic places below and around the flowers.

Make leaves that are appropriate for the flowers; use dark green icing for some and medium green icing for others.

Make light blue forget-me-nots directly on tree (see *DC*, pp. 27f.).

Pipe a No. 46 (plain side up) green ribbon around base of tree. Make leaves horizontally just above green ribbon.

SPRING FLOWERS

Make up five large white buttercream Easter lilies according to the new method on p. 14.

Make up seven daffodils according to the method taught in BCF, pp. 165f. Use squares of absorbent paper towel on No. 7 nail. Make petals with No. 125 yellow cone. Form trumpet with variegated yellow and orange icing in a No. 125 cone. Make pistil and six stamens with yellow No. 2 cone. Form top edge of trumpet with a No. 101s orange cone. Place daffodils with their paper squares on crumpled paper towel to speed drying and shape flowers differently.

Cover a 9-by-13-inch cake with light blue icing. (Fig. 75, p. 154.)

Make arrangement of stems and leaves for lilies and daffodils, using the illustration as a model and referring as necessary to BCF, pp. 165ff. and 90f. If necessary, *freeze* dried lilies and daffodils for five minutes before removing them from paper and placing them in arrangement.

Remember to add a cone of very *soft* white buttercream icing to the base of each Easter lily after it is placed on the cake. Smooth the soft cone of icing into the base of the lily with a moist brush. Brush some very light green liquid vegetable color on the base of each lily.

Fold a piece of parchment or waxed paper in the middle and cut a pattern for the white flower bowl; it will be shaped the same on both sides when it is opened. Press pattern lightly against the crusted blue icing of the cake top. Lift pattern away.

Form white flower bowl with very *soft* white buttercream icing and a No. 5 cone. Make top rim of bowl cover bottoms of flower stems and daffodil leaves, and make rim thicker by going over it several times. Shape and smooth bowl with a moist brush.

Finish top, base borders, and corners with No. 5 roping made with soft light blue icing.

ROSE CLOCK

Cover a 10-inch cake on a 12-inch baseboard with white icing. (Fig. 76, p. 154.)

Make a template for clock face with paper and pencil. Place template on top of crusted icing and punch through pencil lines at intervals with a straight or T-pin. Remove template.

Drop No. 2 dark green icing on lines formed by pin to create Roman numerals.

Using No. 101s cone and dark pink icing, make tiny rosebuds directly on cake (3-D roses) at ends of stems. Have some buds opened more than others, depending upon space available.

Add sepals and leaves with ⅛-inch V-cone of medium green icing.

Drop circle of No. 3 dark brown icing so that it overlaps base of rose stems.

Drop hour hand with No. 4 dark green cone and minute hand with No. 2 dark green cone. Add narrow ⅜-inch V-cone medium green leaf to minute hand. Add wide leaf, made with same V-cone, to hour hand.

Place a triple-toned pink nail rose made with a No. 104 cone, at the center of the clock.

Using a No. 27 cone of light brown icing, encircle the top border of cake.

Form inside base border with No. 27 light brown shell work. Finish outside base border with No. 13 light brown shell work.

If you need further help, please study nail roses, *DC*, pp. 49ff.; 3-D roses, *BCF*, pp. 126ff.

MEDLEY OF FLOWERS

Ice a 10-inch square, one-layer cake with white icing. (Fig. 77, p. 155.)

After icing is crusted, divide each side of cake by thirds and make slight indentations at top edge. Hold a long thread or fine string tightly between both hands and press diagonal indentations in crusted icing to form diamond pattern.

Make flowers in each full and half-space as indicated in chart. Read left to right.

WHOLE DIAMOND	HALF DIAMOND
1. Double Perennial Sweet Peas (pp. 120ff.)	1. Nail Rose (*DC*, p. 46, pp. 49ff.)
2. Ageratum (p. 40)	2. Pansy (pp. 156f.)
3. Blanket Flower (pp. 154ff.)	3. Full Carnation (pp. 175f.)
4. Three-D Rose (pp. 126ff.)	4. Christmas Rose (pp. 182ff.)

WHOLE DIAMOND	HALF DIAMOND
5. Bleeding Hearts (pp. 34ff.)	5. Lilies of the Valley (DC, pp. 43ff.)
6. Bluebells (p. 29)	6. Cottage Pink (pp. 153f.)
7. Calla Lily (pp. 215ff.)	7. Daffodil (pp. 165f.)
8. Half-Nasturtium (pp. 194ff.)	8. Dahlia (pp. 166ff.)
9. Orchid (pp. 221f.)	9. Daisies (pp. 80f.)
10. Forsythia (pp. 73f.)	10. Dogwood (pp. 158ff.)
11. Hyacinths (p. 15)	11. Gardenia (pp. 25ff.)
12. Iris (pp. 205ff.)	12. Monkshood (pp. 134f.)

If you need help in making flowers, please consult *BCF* unless *DC* is inserted before the page numbers indicated on the chart. You can substitute other flowers or repeat flowers if you wish.

If you want to insert an inscription, you may omit some flowers and write a message in their place.

Holding a No. 102 white cone in a vertical position, form ribbons in white icing along diagonal indentations which divide flowers (or flowers and message), and around top border. Make two upside-down Vs with same ribbon on each side of cake, and make a vertical ribbon at each corner.

Pipe No. 5 golden brown roping around bottom border.

Cut cake along ribbon lines when dividing it. Serve half-diamond pieces to those guests who are dieting.

TULIP CAKE

The tulip cake may be used for Easter, for a birthday, or as a centerpiece.

Ice a 10-inch cake with white icing. (Fig. 78, p. 171.) Place it on a 12-inch baseboard that is iced light brown or chocolate.

FIG. 78 (78C, p. 155)

Make up orchid, pink, and yellow No. 104 cones for half-tulips. Form eight half-tulips of each color on liquid ice cans or metal surfaces and place them in freezer for five or ten minutes.

Evenly space twelve marks in the icing about 3 inches from the top center. Make twelve more evenly spaced marks in the icing on the side and near the base of the cake.

At the top of the cake, place an extended back petal of No. 104 yellow icing in a left diagonal position at one of the marks. Continue to the right in the same way with pink and then with orchid. Continue in this way.

Continue the same routine on the side of the cake, except that all petals should be straight up and down. Make every other one lower.

Take tulips out of freezer and remove them from the metal surfaces with a thin, sharp, cold knife. Place them on the appropriate petals on the cake. (Now they will look more like full tulips.)

Add No. 3 green stems. Add ¼-inch V-cone green tulip leaves.

Using a No. 3 brown cone, make stretched rope around top border, dots around inside base border, and modified rope around outside base border.

Add an appropriate message at the top center of the cake if you wish.

If you need help, please study stretched rope, p. 31; modified rope, p. 31; extended back petal, *BCF*, pp. 115f.; half-tulips, *BCF*, pp. 131ff.

ARTIST AT WORK

Bake a cake in an oval pan, or bake a 9-inch-by-13-inch rectangular cake and trim it to an oval shape. Carve out a finger space in the palette-shaped cake. (Fig. 79, p. 173.)

Cover the cake with white icing.

On waxed-paper squares make some yellow-orange and brown mums, yellow daisies with brown centers and a white daisy with a yellow center, and yellow gaillardias painted with red vegetable color. Using shallow nail No. 8 and waxed paper, make some yellow marigolds.

While flowers are being frozen for five minutes or more, make three long stems of light green fern with No. 2 cone for stems and ⅛-inch V-cone for leaves.

Remove frozen flowers from waxed papers and place around top of cake. Add appropriate medium green leaves.

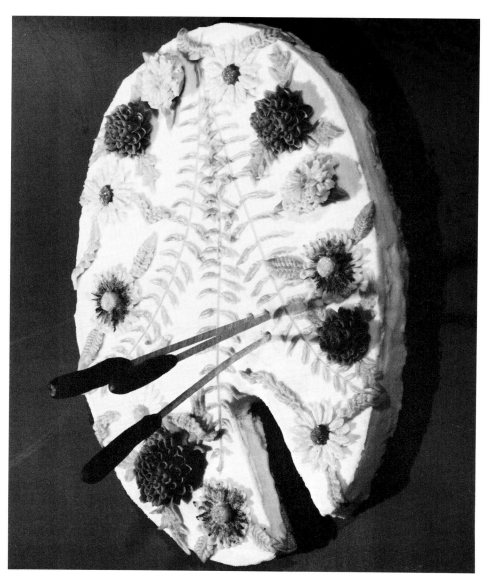

FIG. 79 (79C, p. 156)

Punch three holes in the top of the cake near the finger space. Cut three green soft-drink straws so that they vary in length.

Thicken a small amount of buttercream decorating icing with sifted powdered sugar until it has the consistency of putty. Add brown paste coloring and a touch of red paste coloring to the thickened icing until it is the reddish-brown color of cattails. Form icing by hand around the straws to form cattails, and then place straw stems in holes prepared for them.

If you need help in making particular flowers or leaves, please study BCF: mums (chrysanthemums), pp. 82ff.; daisies, pp. 80f.; gaillardias, p. 154; marigolds (calendulas), pp. 187f.; fern, pp. 69f.; leaves, pp. 41ff.

CHRYSANTHEMUM CAKE

Place a single 6-inch layer of cake on top of a three-layer, 10-inch cake. Cover the complete cake with white icing and put it on a 12-inch baseboard. (Fig. 80, p. 175.)

Make three layers of No. 5 very soft white beads around the side of the 6-inch layer cake. Form top border of 10-inch cake with No. 5 beadwork.

Mark top border at ten evenly spaced intervals. At each of these marks draw No. 4 green stems from top to base of cake. On each stem make single and divided chrysanthemum leaves with ¼-inch V-cone of green icing.

On top of 6-inch layer form a five-section pattern of leaves that start in the center and finally overlap the beadwork.

Make inside and outside base borders with very soft white No. 5 beadwork. Form center base border with brown No. 5 beadwork.

Using a No. 7 nail and squares of waxed paper, make the lower petals of each chrysanthemum with a No. 79 tube and the upper and center petals with a No. 81 tube. Open the centers of the tube openings with a strong steel pin or similar instrument. (More icing at the center supports the edges of the petals. Softer buttercream icing can be used; this makes the decorator's work easier.)

Make six orange-yellow, five two-toned brown and tan, and five combination brown and tan with orange-yellow in center. Freeze mums for five minutes, remove them from papers, and place them on cake.

FIG. 80 (80C, p. 156)

Place one orange-yellow in center. Put the brown and yellow combinations around the center and between the leaves. Place brown mums and yellow mums alternately on stems at edge of 10-inch cake.

When mums begin to thaw, bring lowest layer of petals down slightly for a more natural appearance.

For more help in making chrysanthemums and leaves, please study BCF, pp. 82ff. and 46ff.

APPENDIX A

INDEX FOR CHAPTERS I-V

APPENDIX B

INDEX OF CREATIONS BY TITLE FOR CHAPTERS VI-XIX

APPENDIX C

INDEX OF CREATIONS BY
FLOWERS AND GREENERY FOR CHAPTERS VI-XIX

APPENDIX D

GENERAL INDEX OF
27, 28, AND 29 CREATIONS BY TITLE

APPENDIX E

187

APPENDIX F

BUTTERCREAM DECORATING ICING

SMALL BATCH
Note: All ingredients should be at room temperature.

2 *cups pure vegetable shortening (A high-ratio shortening such as Sweetex* gives best results.)*

a) Mix shortening by hand or on *slowest* speed (using paddle) on machine until smooth. (At each stage mix batch until it is smooth, but mix as little as possible in order to keep air bubbles to a minimum.)

4 *cups powdered sugar*
salt to taste
cornstarch†

Note: Measure powdered sugar before sifting it.

b) Sift powdered sugar and salt (and cornstarch, if it is used during hot, humid weather).
c) Add *half* of the sifted mixture to the shortening.
d) Mix by hand or on slow speed (if a machine is used) until smooth.
e) Stop mixing, scrape mix down with a spatula or plastic scraper, and mix until smooth again.

1 *tablespoon cold water*
butter flavor and vanilla, or other flavor, to taste

f) Stop mixing, and add water and flavors to icing.
g) Mix by hand or on slow speed until smooth.
h) Stop mixing and add rest of the sifted, dry ingredients to icing (see c).
i) Mix by hand or on slow speed until smooth.
j) Stop mixing and scrape icing down with a spatula or plastic scraper.
k) Mix once more by hand or on slow speed until smooth.

*Sweetex may be purchased in large quantities (50 lbs. or more) from bakery and restaurant supply houses. It may also be bought in small amounts by mail from Maid of Scandinavia Company, 3245 Raleigh Avenue, Minneapolis, Minnesota 55416, and from Kitchen Glamor, Inc., 26770 Grand River Avenue, Detroit, Michigan 48240.
†During hot, humid weather use 2 to 4 tablespoons of cornstarch.

l)   Stop mixing.
m)   Put icing in a tightly sealed plastic, glass or metal container, and store in a cool place.

Note: When stored at a reasonable temperature, 60 to 70 degrees F., icing will keep for several weeks. Do *not* place icing in a refrigerator except under unusual conditions. It should be at room temperature when it is used.

n)   When icing is to be used, work it smooth with a spatula or table knife before putting it into a decorating cone.
o)   When using tubes with very small openings, thin icing with a few drops of water.
p)   If icing is too soft because of difference in materials or temperature, add *sifted* powdered sugar.
q)   If icing is too stiff, add a little cold water.

LARGE BATCH

Note: All ingredients should be at room temperature.

3 *lbs. pure vegetable shortening (A high-ratio shortening such as Sweetex gives best results.)*

a)   Mix shortening by hand or on *slowest* speed (using paddle) on machine until smooth. (At each stage mix batch until it is smooth, but mix as little as possible in order to keep air bubbles to a minimum.)

6 *lbs. powdered sugar*
½ *oz. salt*
cornstarch*

b)   Sift powdered sugar and salt (and cornstarch, if it is used during hot, humid weather).
c)   Add *half* of the sifted mixture to the shortening.
d)   Mix by hand or on slow speed (if a machine is used) until smooth.
e)   Stop mixing, scrape mix down with a spatula or plastic scraper, and mix until smooth again.

5 *oz. water*
butter flavor and vanilla, or other flavor, to taste

f)   Stop mixing, and add water and flavors to icing.
g)   Mix by hand or on slow speed until smooth.
h)   Stop mixing and add rest of the sifted, dry ingredients to icing (see c).
i)   Mix by hand or on slow speed until smooth.
j)   Stop mixing and scrape icing down with a spatula or plastic scraper.
k)   Mix once more by hand or on slow speed until smooth.
l)   Stop mixing.
m)   Continue as for small batch.

---

*During hot, humid weather use 6 to 12 oz. cornstarch and increase powdered sugar to 6¼ lbs.